ANALYZE ANYONE ON SIGHT

Dylan Clearfield

Copyright ©2017 by Prism Thomas
G. Stempien Publishing Company

Second revised edition

ISBN 978-0-930472-26-9

Editorial offices at New Quay, Wales, UK
All rights reserved

CONTENTS

INTRODUCTION

FIRST STEPS TO IDENTIFICATION

INTRODUCING A SMILE

READING THE FULL FACE

BODY LANGUAGE SELF DEFENSE

MEETING STRANGERS

CON ARTISTS

FIST, THUMB AND FOREARM POWER

HANDSHAKES

HANDY GESTURES

MICRO-EXPRESSIONS (HOW TO READ THEM LIVE)

SIGNS OF FLIRTING

PEOPLE TO AVOID

REAL TIME ANALYSIS

FINALLY

ONE MORE THING

INTRODUCTION

Any person can be analyzed on sight. This book tells you how, using the latest 21st century methods. It's perfect for someone on a first date, at a job interview, or any time a new person comes into your life.

While there are many books on this topic none of them are exactly like this one. This book is filled with "valid" photos which will be used to demonstrate how peoples' true feelings are betrayed by both body and facial language. By "valid" photos it is meant to refer to the photos that **are not** staged and are taken of people in the actual throes of emotion or displaying a specific attitude. This is critical because you will want a "valid" emotion by which to judge the comparisons that you'll be making in real life rather than something that had been faked.

This is truly a how-to book. Use it as you approach the person you are about to meet and judge his or her attitude based on the photos and accompanying description.

There are three other very special features to this book. One of them will give you exact information on flirting techniques and how to decipher the cues being sent your way. This is for all genders.

Another very important feature is one on recognizing people who display psychopathic tendencies. These tendencies can be read as clearly as any other type of non-verbal messages. It is hoped that the reader will recognize the warning signs sent by these people and avoid the people sending them.

Thirdly, a section of this book will be set aside consisting only of photos which you can use in real time to compare to a person you are meeting for the first time – or any time – in order to evaluate his current attitude.

This book was written in a concise and straightforward style for a reason. This is a how-to book which is meant to give the reader the basic information needed to understand and apply the concepts of body language. It therefore lacks the jargon and technicalities that would only overwhelm the basic facts and make the subject even less comprehensible. I have read many books about body language and by the time I reached the second chapter I was usually exhausted from all of the overblown explanations and the usage of unnecessary terminology. In this book you will find the basic facts and the basic concepts which you can then apply to the outside world.

THE SCIENCE INVOLVED

The science of facial language and body language has been around since at least the time of Aristotle and probably a great deal longer. This book relies on the same science in its most updated form. But this book will not weigh down the reader with details of the science itself. It is expected that the reader wants to know information about the meaning of facial and body gestures, but not necessarily the multitude of theories which provide the background for this information.

Again, this book is primarily for the everyday person who wants to be able to know on first glance what to expect from someone he has just met. In a purely social setting this can avoid a certain amount of embarrassment. But in a potentially dangerous setting this type of knowledge can be used to avoid much worse than mere embarrassment. But this information can also be applied to anyone you meet – be it old friend, or whoever – at any time. Moods and dispositions change.

With all of this in mind, it is important to note that despite all of the science that has been brought to bear on this topic the science itself is still not what is called "precise." Even the most sophisticated system on this topic - the Facial Action Coding System - that has been developed to categorize various facial expressions is useful only within the context of the setting in which the expressions are made. For example, a quick glance to the left by a subject can only have meaning in regard to why the subject made a quick glance to that direction. A person cannot dogmatically pronounce that because a person glanced to the left that this automatically means he is being evasive or deceitful. Maybe he'd been asked a self-incriminating question and was simply trying to protect himself by the evasion, if evasion it was. Which I do not automatically accept.

The study of facial and body language isn't like geometry or physics even though these two disciplines have been used for this subject. This is truly a social science and, as an anthropologist, that is how I have evaluated it. It is a science of emotion and of deduction not of mathematical calculations as some have attempted to define it.

And that is where the strength of this report lies. In order to study body and facial language it is critical that the samples be true samples, samples taken of people in the throes of true emotional display and not of staged photographs of people who were instructed as to what emotion to portray for the picture. That's all it would be – a portrayal. An act.

Most of the samples in this work are taken from people caught in their daily lives as they are displaying their emotions in both their body and facial language. The context in which the samples (photos) were taken gives the explanation for the emotion that is being displayed. For example, one photo is of two men having an altercation at a gas station. This lets us know that this is a potentially hostile confrontation and their body language is based on that.

This is not laboratory science but human, on the street, anthropological science. Humans are best studied in their natural environment. And that isn't in a laboratory. It's out in the everyday world.

Because many of the photos were taken on impulse to capture people acting on impulse many of them were made from a distance and a certain amount of enlargement had to be performed. As you know, this can detract from the overall quality of the picture. So please bear with some of the photos which may be of lesser quality. I felt it was more important to capture genuine emotional displays rather than to produce high quality photographs.

I used a hidden, high resolution digital camera. Not an I-phone or a camera with a telescopic lens. Either of these would have attracted unwanted attention and taken away from the "now" of the moment.

Expect to find a lot of humor in this report. Humor is a large part of the human experience and it too is captured in body and facial language. Always keep in mind, this book is not only very useful as a guide to what to expect from your fellow humans but it is also meant to be enjoyable reading.

The examples in this book are taken mainly from people living in Western culture. While there are numerous differences in the meanings of facial and body language between Asian and other cultures that are different from those in the West (North America, most of South and

Central America, Europe, Australia and New Zealand) these aren't relevant to the scope of this work. For example, in some cultures nodding the head means "no" and shaking the head means "yes." Few of us are likely to come across this difference with any regularity.

Again, one purpose of this book is to help the reader analyze a person he'd just met on sight. This will help you to both keep out of trouble and gravitate toward people who will be beneficial in your life.

A NOTE ABOUT THE PHOTOS

As already mentioned, most of the photographs have been taken of average people taking part in daily life. That is why some of the photos are not as clear as one would like. Another very important point is that none of the photos have been photo-shopped. Because of this, some of the edited photos might seem a little crude. The reason for this is to maintain the integrity of the photos. It was deemed important to use the original photos untouched in all cases. If one of the edited photos would have been photo-shopped it would have been a case of creating a new photo. If that had been the purpose, drawings could have been used instead of photos. Once again, I chose to sacrifice esthetics for integrity.

Below is an example of an edited non-photo-shopped photo. In this case, edited means that it is a real photo of a real person where the head was removed to protect identity. Only the body movement was important to this photo. That wasn't changed.

But in no case has the body or facial language in any photo been altered or tampered with in the slightest. On occasion a whimsical face has been drawn in where the original could not be used by request. This was intended to add a little humor.

A WORD ABOUT OVERALL FACE AND BODY SHAPES

There are many older theories that link the shape of a person's face or the type of body type he possesses with the type of personality this implies. A very famous work about body type analysis in the early 1920's used these criteria for promoting the most absurd of ideas. For example, it was stated that because the Irish are supposedly known to be heavy drinkers they often get into barroom brawls. Because of this, they have developed hard, square jaws to withstand their many drunken frays.

In a like manner, heavy, round-faced individuals are supposed to be jovial or jolly. It isn't really explained why being overweight leads to being jolly other than displaying that the person in question has enough of an income to dine wherever and whenever he desired.

None of those comparisons of body or facial type are scientifically provable and are in fact in many cases insulting. Accepting the concept of the hard-jawed Irishman wouldn't be much different from saying that the reason why light skinned people are light skinned is because they spend so much time sleeping inside due to laziness so that they have developed an albino pallor.

While many people would like to believe that they can decipher a personality type by simply observing the body type it is a pursuit that isn't valid.

First Steps to Identification

One thing this chapter is about is how to make an instant reading of a person you have just met by decoding the signals being given by feet, leg and arm placement. Have you ever noticed that usually the first things you see about a new person are the way the feet, legs and arms are positioned? Sometimes this is because he is either approaching you from the distance or you are observing him from a distance. If that should be the case for you, the information that follows will help you determine what to expect from this individual **BEFORE** you meet him.

The photo that follows is a very common stance among men and one you must've seen very often as you approach an acquaintance.

In this example, let it be assumed that he has seen you and notices your approach. Note the feet right away. One of them is pointing directly at you and the other is pointing off to his right. This is clearly a sign that he is undecided. Basic body language tells us that the feet give indication where the mind is directing us. Sometimes the mind isn't sure. When that's the case you have a foot placement like the one above. This person is not completely convinced that this will be a successful event.

But when reading body or facial language a person must look to other signs for verification or for nullification. One sign is very slim evidence. Maybe the person in the above photo just naturally stands that way. But note below:

Arms folded like this are very telling. In this case they verify what the feet have already suggested. This person is "closed off." Not only are his arms folded but they're tightly folded at near chest level. He is definitely on guard and not open to sharing at the moment.

This is a critical feature to always look for. Whenever body parts are folded and held tightly together that is often a sign of a person who is protecting his privacy, assuming always that he isn't standing this way as protection from the cold.

BUT – let's take a look at this face. What does that tell us? This is the smile.

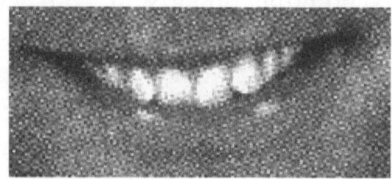

It appears to be a smile. His mouth seems happy to see you. But this can sometimes be deceptive. Do the eyes match his enthusiasm?

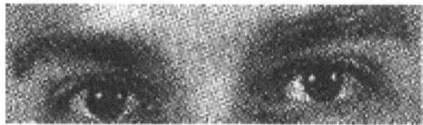

For a smile to be genuine, the eyes must be "smiling" too. Smiling is a feature that is shown by a wide "blooming" of the eyes. This in turn causes lines of cheer, as I term them, to radiate from the sides of the eyes as well as beneath them. The eyes pictured above **ARE NOT** smiling eyes. They are bland and somewhat staring.

These eyes seem stiff and unimpressed. They seem to perfectly match his lower body language. He is reserved and uncertain. While his eyes are "normal" they are not friendly. Later in this book we will examine "abnormal" eyes which belong to psychopaths and with them, this is the primary facial language you will need to know.

The person above is not a psychopath, he simply does not seem overly eager for the upcoming meeting. I later learned this from him.

Let's move on to a second subject. Keep in mind that this same body and facial language can be applied to women in this example. There are some subtle differences but these will be noted when they come up.

There isn't a lot to say about the posture shown below that doesn't seem already obvious. This person is not only distant but unfriendly. Her arms are very tightly folded and her legs are twisted together at the knees. But her feet placement tells you the most. They display a desire to be left alone. She might just as well be wearing a sign that reads, *Stay away from me!*

Put all three signs together and they add up to a person who doesn't want to see anybody at that time.

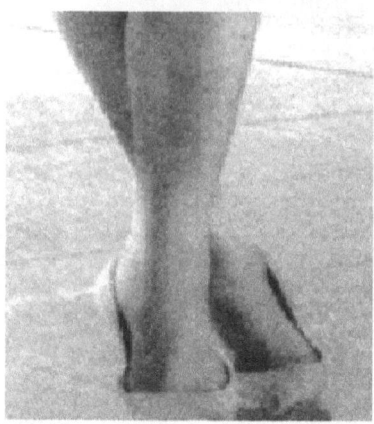

AS CLEAR A WARNING TO STAY AWAY AS YOU'LL EVER GET!

Let's turn to some body language that is more challenging, yet relatively common. The person pictured below has seen your approach. He faces you and extends an open-palmed hand in greeting. He even has one of his feet pointing toward you in anticipation of your arrival. But there's something contradictory about his stance. Can

you guess what it might be?

Look closely at his left leg (your point of view). He is actually stepping backward. This is a sign of desired escape. With all of his other body features he is welcoming you, but with this one he is moving back from you. How would you read this case?

You would get more information by analyzing his facial language (missing here unfortunately due to request). You know the smile to look for if he is truly happy to see you. Is it there? Unfortunately, this subject would not allow his face to be shown. Why not use another subject? Because of the rarity of this body language. It's extremely unusual for a person to reveal such conflicting body language. Staged photos are not used in this book.

There are some basic features to look for when considering the legs and the feet insofar as indicators of a person's mood or disposition. If the legs are straight and parallel while a person is standing that indicates someone who is confident yet friendly. If the legs are spread far apart this reveals someone who is open and friendly. If they are only partially separated this implies self-assurance. Legs that are tightly held together show fear, tension – mostly in women – and self-doubt.

When a male is in a sitting position and he keeps his legs slightly apart this implies someone who is relaxed and self-possessed. If the person is female this body language also denotes a relaxed person but also one who is open to a closer relationship. See the photos below.

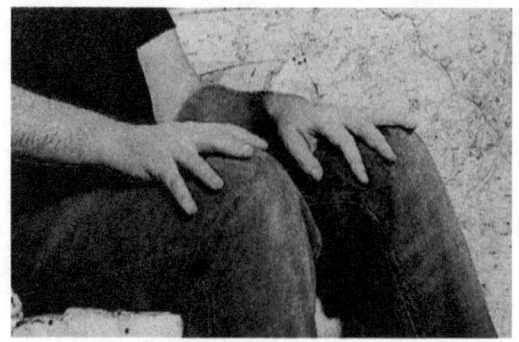

Self-possessed male, but palms are turned down (not open) and tense.

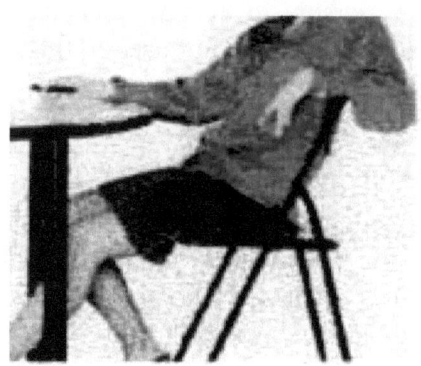

Female comfortable with self (note dangling hand).

In the above photo, these two people aren't quite sure how to proceed. They each have one foot pointed toward the other – a positive sign – and one foot pointing away from the other as in preparing to flee. In addition, they both have the open leg stance which presumes a desire for closeness. A good guess would be that they have just met, are attracted, but aren't yet sure.

Once again, the feet point in the direction in which the mind wants us to go when in another's presence. But when alone, the positioning of the feet also gives clues as to the current state of mind of their owner. If the feet are parallel this person is alert to his environment and, if he is with someone, he is paying attention to the person he is with. If he's alone and his feet point inward this is a sign of insecurity. If they point outward they denote self-assuredness.

Remember that when reading the placement of the feet they should be read differently depending on whether the person is alone or with someone else. The photo below seems to be a stance exclusively performed by women and it displays what it looks like it displays: utter confusion bordering on panic.

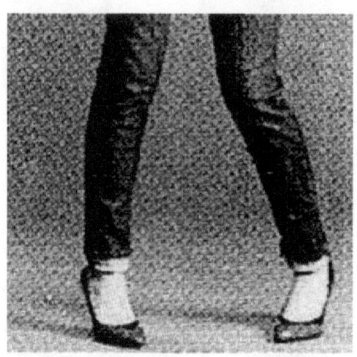

The feet do not know which way to go and the twisted condition of the legs compounds the dilemma. You can imagine the facial expression that would accompany this stance! Look below to see:

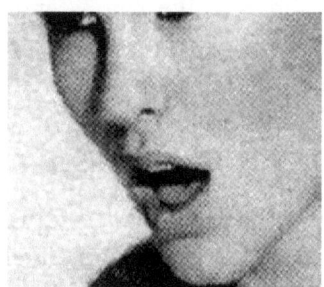

Or…

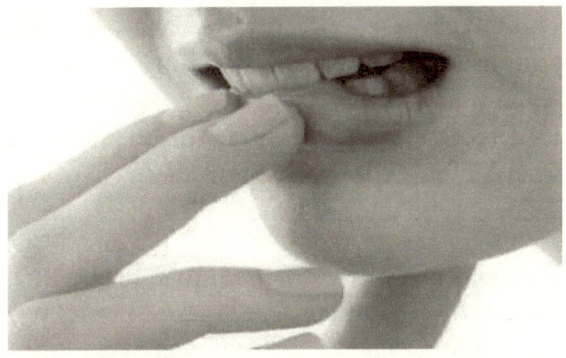

If you are watching two or more people from a distance and would like to know what is taking place between them, note their stance and the positions of their feet. Which way are the feet pointing and how are the legs being placed. As an example, study the photo of the two men in the forefront below.

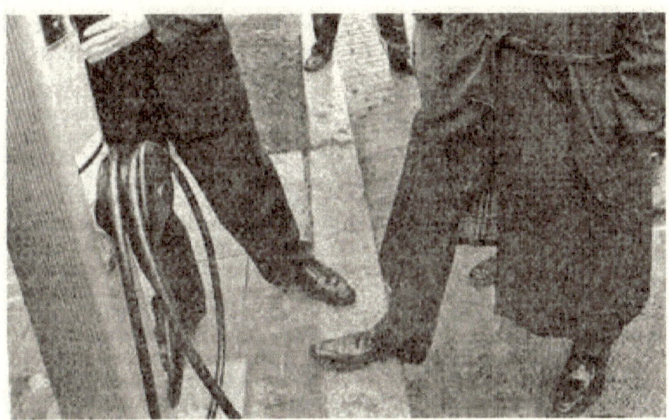

These are two men at an air hose. Even though one of the men's feet is partially hidden, the direction it is pointing can be determined. Both the placement of the feet and legs denote this as a hostile confrontation. In fact, each man had wanted to use this air hose at the same time and a row took place.

Look at the feet. Both men have one foot pointed squarely at the air hose as if claiming possession of it. Look at each man's other foot, however. It is pointed in an indefinite direction from the other person as if uncertain how to proceed. Not only that, these two men seem comfortable to keep their distance.

This photo is of two men who had become involved in a heated confrontation but would like to quickly extricate themselves from it. The altercation was eventually avoided and the two men went on their way.

In an unrelated way, here is one very important point to remember. People generally have a more favorable opinion of you if you are standing to their right. Some experts feel that this only applies to observers of you who are right handed and that a lefty would rather see you on his left. However, since the majority of people are right handed and if you must choose a side on which to stand without knowing the observer's "handedness" your best choice is the right for obvious reasons.

My belief is that no matter what the observer's "handedness" is it is more beneficial to stand to his right. Why? Because most people seem to favor looking to the right with their eyes and it is easier and more natural for them.

You can tell a great deal about a person before coming within twenty feet of him. Look at the stance that is being taken and **all of the features** that accompany it.

This woman is highly approachable. Her arms are open before her and her palms are wide and inviting. Her legs are also slightly apart and her feet are in a friendly position. Particularly note the palms. Open palms are a

sign of welcome or of honesty and openness.

The next photo shows arms limp before the body, denoting uncertainty. If they were held out to the side of the body it would imply openness and assuredness. But in this case she is waiting to make a judgment before committing.

When a person touches another's arm this is a sign of closeness or an invitation of such.

Touching your own arm doesn't count.

Shaking hands is something most of us do. The first example is a warm hand clasp with something added. The back of the hand is also being touched and this act causes a type of binding or closeness between the two people involved. It's more than a simple handshake. But it can turn into a clutch of control if held too long and too tightly.

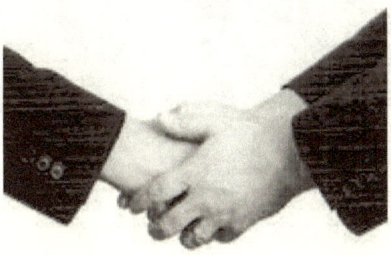

Note the handshake below. These two people are doing something more akin to grappling than shaking hands. Excuses are again asked for the quality of the photo which was taken with great difficulty.

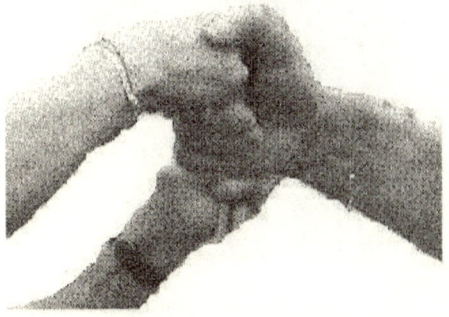

People often use their hands for signaling. Standing with their hands **in** their pockets can mean one thing while standing with hands **outside** the pockets can mean something quite different. And there is a very subtle yet important difference between where their **thumbs** are positioned.

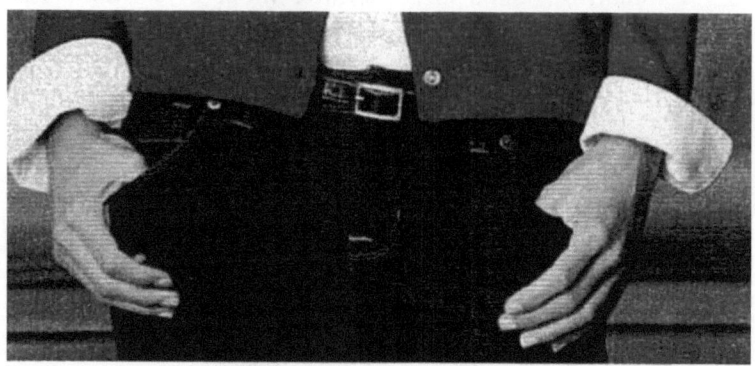

In the above picture, the thumbs are in the side pockets, signaling a lack of desire for open communication. This stance applies to both genders.

Outside the pocket.

Next, the thumb is clearly outside the pocket almost as if it is on display. This is a sign of confidence and of someone who may have a particularly high opinion of himself. However, because he isn't insecure he is open to open communication. This is also true of women. See...

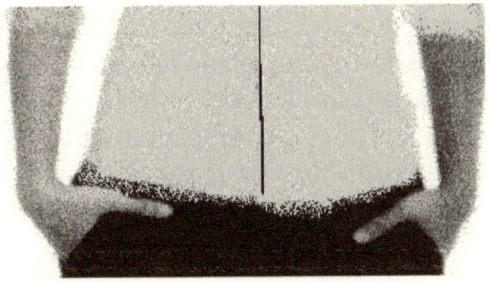

Women do something else with their hands which is more common among females and less so among males.

In both the above and below photos the fingers are clearly pointing toward a specific area to receive attention. Compare the above photo more closely with the one below and see if you can spot the abnormality.

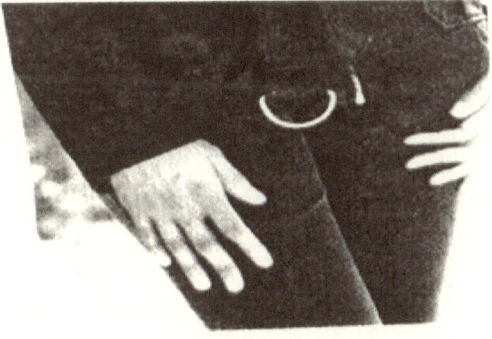

The photo directly above is staged by an advertiser meant to confuse the viewer. The lower body portion of this photo is female. The hands are in a specifically female pose. But the left hand only (as from the reader's point of

25

view) belongs to a male! It's a very old device used by the advertising industry. Many photos in ads that are supposed to be of women are in fact of men who look like women. Also, many photos have a combination of male and female features. The reason for this is to subliminally attract the reader of a certain psychological mindset. (This is a staged catalogue photo used for demonstration)

The next photo is of a female who is in a legs apart pose which conveys a very mixed message.

What's odd about this pose is that the woman is blocking with her right hand the part of her body that her left hand (mostly hidden) is directing the viewer toward. It is clearly meant to tease the viewer. Some people, however, find this type of teasing arousing. Overall, she is very approachable.

Below is a similar pose made by a male but in this case it is the pose of someone brimming with self-confidence. He is showing off and knows it. This is a typical pose of the so-called alpha male. Ironic how it mimics the female counterpart.

Women generally do not sit like this for reasons of modesty or else they use their hands or something else as a shield. However, if shielding does occur, the legs apart pose is still an attraction for one's interests.

The legs, arms and feet are also very active even when the person is seated.

(face omitted by request)

The happy fellow seems quite secure. Leaning back in the chair with arms linked behind the head is one of the most open and secure poses a person can take. It would be a surprise if this person were anything but jovial when approached.

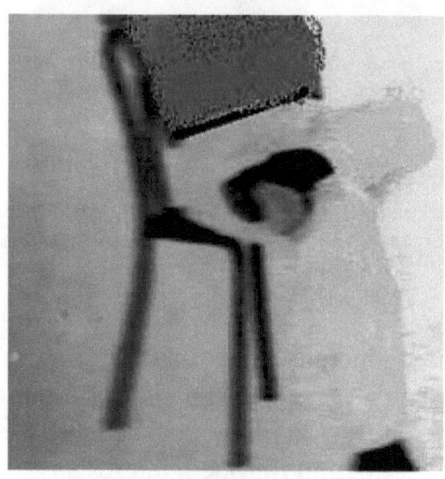

He probably would not have a leg crossed over the top of his knee in a way so that the sole of his shoe is fully exposed like the man above. In some Mid East countries this is considered such an insult that it could put the person sitting in this way in severe personal danger. True! In America it is mixed signal but it usually is used for blocking. It would not fit with the hands joined behind the head pose.

Incidentally, the above type of leg crossing that is horizontal to the knee is a very masculine trait as well as one of mixed meaning. Women seldom use this pose and when they do it could be considered mannish. It would be as if a man crossed his legs like in the photo below.

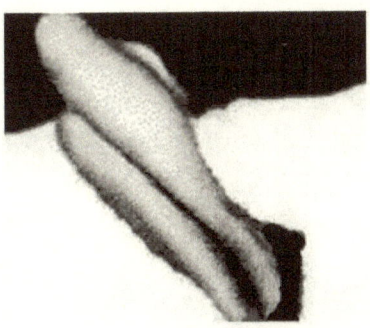

The type of female leg crossing in the photo just shown is extremely sensual and immensely alluring. Ironically, outstretched legs are commonly a sign of distancing oneself from other people except in the above instance. Also, being held so tightly together they would usually signal blocking or un-openness. Not in this case, though. It is the proverbial exception to the rule.

Below is an example of using outstretched legs to both physically and emotionally acquire distance.

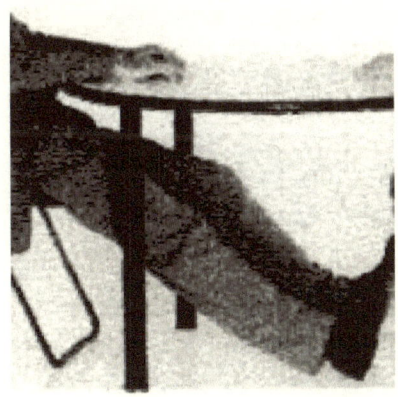

Women do this as well. But women tend to do it more by sitting farther back into a chair than by stretching out their legs.

Another look at leg crossing gives us what can only be considered a tortuous contortion of the legs. A person in this position is clearly under immediate stress who is caught in a position of enforced attendance and is ready to flee at a moments notice. That's what is depicted in the following photo.

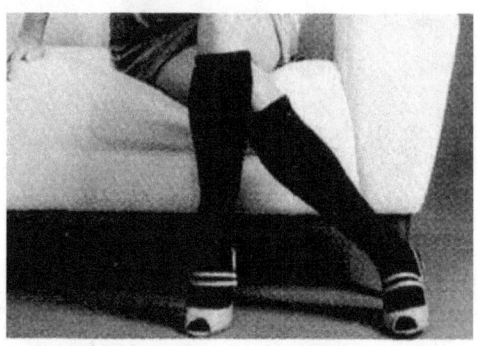

Notice the position of her feet and the painful angle at which her outstretched leg is bent. She even has a hand perched on the seat beside her, ready to propel herself away.

A truism about leg crossing to be mindful of: if the person you are interested in has her legs crossed TOWARD you this implies openness towards you, but if her legs are pointed away from you this means disinterest. This has proved to be accurate though a rather well worn concept.

There are many times when the mere positioning of a body part is so uncomfortable of appearance that it is clear for anyone to see that the person is under some form of stress.

The above twining of hands seems painful. So does the example in the photo below.

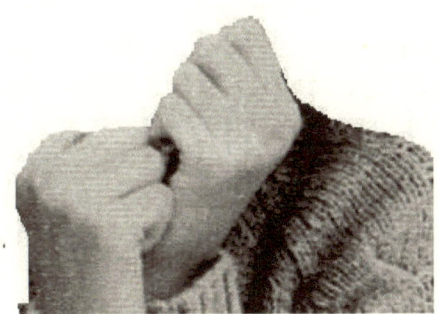

The next picture is a little different. Many people consider this a relaxed posture of the hands. But in reality it is a pose locked in tension. There is one simple test of this. Separate the two hands and see how they look individually when not twined together. They are in the form of hooked claws. Hooked claws are not the sign of a relaxed hand.

This **IS NOT** a position of relaxed comfort!

Arms folded across the chest are typically considered to be a sign of a lack of openness. But the type of arm fold in the photo below takes this one level farther. This person really doesn't want any interpersonal contact. This person seems to be literally fending off any attempts at communication. Looks painful, doesn't it? (Or is he just showing off his cuff link?)

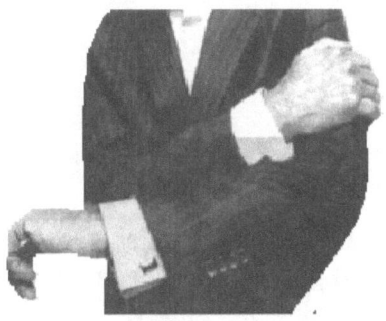

The general rule is that postures that create sharp angles out of crossed body parts denote some form of emotional pain or anger. It is a sign to approach with caution no matter the expression on the face. One more example....

The features just shown are what a person is most likely to observe at first glance upon approaching someone for the first time. Reading a person's stance and the way he holds his arms and legs along with various other body movements will give an important first impression. Next, examine the face. This will add much needed details.

Introducing a Smile

First, an important reminder about the hazards of relying upon staged photographs when performing this type of body and facial language study. Please bear with the repetition.

Below is a prime example of the serious pitfalls that arise from using made up pictures. Below is a staged photo of a person who is supposed to be happily surprised. He is told to mimic the expression that he thinks he would exhibit if he was happily surprised. Below is the result.

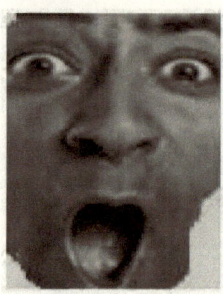

Note the bulging eyes and the wide open mouth. If you were led to believe that this is the actual typical expression of a person who is happily surprised, you would have been badly misled. It is actually the look of sheer terror!

Below is a photograph taken of a person from the distance while he was in the process of truly being happily surprised. Note the difference.

Sorry for the poor quality, but sometimes quality of picture has to be sacrificed for integrity of the emotion captured. This man was photographed from a <u>great</u> distance. While the mouth of the man in the above photo is indeed wide open – his teeth are showing – and his eyes are initially closed. Note the difference in the way that each man widens his mouth. The second man IS happily surprised. Why would he close his eyes? I don't know. It is a natural human reaction, proven repeatedly. Not this:

Since we're reviewing this pair of eyes: do you notice something peculiar about them? Do these eyes seem happy? They don't seem happy to me. In fact, these are

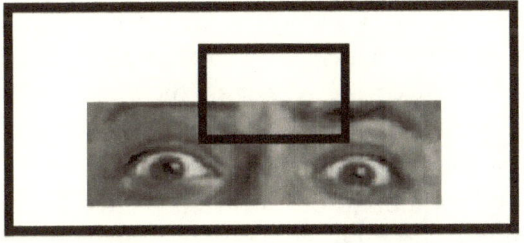

scared eyes. Almost terrified. How do I know?

One clue is found in the area between the eyes that is within the small black square above. See how the skin is pinched together? That is a typical sign of fear or, to a lesser degree, distress. So how ironic is it that a man who was told to simulate a person who was elated with joy should actually reveal a pair of eyes that showed signs of terror?

This demonstrates that not only can a staged photograph give you the completely wrong expression for a particular emotion it can also give an expression for an emotion that is the direct opposite of what it is supposed to represent.

You can easily note this distressed expression on your own face. I often have seen it on mine. When in distress the area between one's eyes becomes compressed. All you need to do is look into a mirror when having a bad day. I hope you do not see the "pinched eyes" expression often. It's a facial expression shared by both genders.

However, it is an expression that most people easily interpret. It's your way of unconsciously saying, "I don't need any more stress." Unfortunately, many people ignore this simple plea for a little peace and quiet.

(Once again, about my photographs): photographs are taken of unsuspecting people from a distance as they engage in genuine activity in order to study the true expressions and body language they are experiencing for the event through which they are going. No, this isn't stalking. They – or the owner of the rights – are always contacted later and informed of the situation and can request that their photos not be used. I have yet to have that request. Although on occasion I have been asked to not reveal the face at which time I usually draw in a pleasantly comical caricature for humorous effect. The staged pictures are with permission from printed sources and most often from the National Archives.

One final point about staged versus genuine examples of emotional signaling. Even animals can be used for ulterior purposes when being posed before the camera to elicit certain responses. For example: which of the two dogs pictured below do you think is REALLY happy?

OR...

There are many things that make people happy and many reasons to smile. What do you think it is that could make an aging but still spry looking woman smile like this?

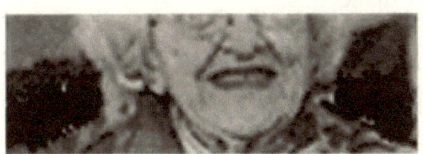

Did her daughter just have baby? Or maybe this woman is smiling because it is her 53rd wedding anniversary. Or she's just won a Pulitzer.

While all of these events may have happened and have made this person very happy, they are not the immediate reason for her smile.

This is what makes this kindly appearing, grandmotherly like woman so very happy:

Fun for the whole family! A new shotgun. It seems that sitting in a rocker and knitting would be a little too tame for this well armed woman. I just hope her glasses prescription is up to date.

A smile is a very powerful expression. Especially a smile that is genuine. It's a simple fact that people are charmed by a smile. However, a faked smile can easily be deciphered by most people and this could be perceived as a form of deceit, depending on the type of smile. Since people generally don't like to be deceived, this will not leave a very good impression. That's how the emotions work beneath the surface, or what most people call the subconscious.

But not all forced smiles are necessarily negative. In some cases they can be placating and meant to make the person it is shared with feel better by making him think that the person smiling is feeling okay, even though he's not. Like when you might be suffering from a migraine headache, but you smile through it anyway. It's a nice gesture, but a gesture that can normally be decoded at the subconscious level. However, it is read as a caring gesture – even though deceptive – because it is meant to make the recipient of it feel relief.

The other type of forced smile isn't so well received. It's the one we've all seen which says, "I really don't like you but I'm going to smile as if I like you in hopes that you will be misled by the deception." Very few people are ever misled by the deception and can decipher the phoniness of the smile.

Here is what a FORCED smile looks like:

It isn't easy to tell that it's fake just by looking at the mouth (eyes are shown below). The eyes are the critical factor. They are always the critical factor when determining the trustworthiness of a smile. Although in this case the mouth is set in such a way that the teeth are gritted which is not usually a sign of good will.

But, as most often, the eyes have it. These are not the eyes of a happy smile. For one thing – they're staring too much for that.

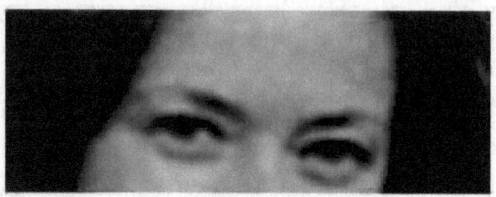

What tells us that these are not happy eyes? Mostly the blandness of the eyes. If this was a true smile the outsides of the eyes would be widened and radiating what I call "smile lines" and others might simply call wrinkles. But the entire facial area lacks the openness of a true smile.

Next is a real smile. The kind of a smile that says, "I'm really happy!" For this smile, a photograph was taken of a cleric who had just been promoted to a higher office. Notice the sheer delight in his face.

His mouth is showing genuine happiness. But it's the eyes that beam his true delight although difficult to see in this picture.

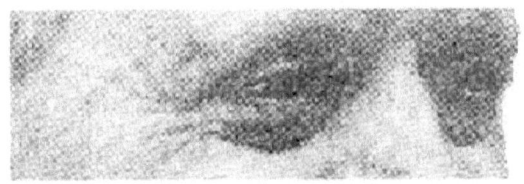

Notice two things about the area around his right eye (viewer's left). One feature is what could be called crow's feet spreading outward from the corners. These are actually signs of real happiness. His face is stretched to the limit with this emotion. Then look at the puffy, baggy section beneath his eye. It is also a sign of his upper face being stretched to its limit with happiness. These might seem to be odd signs of happiness but in photo after photo of people smiling with bursting happiness those same features are there.

Do you think this might be just because the man pictured is older and these are natural wrinkles? Look at the next photo which was taken of a girl not far out of her teens.

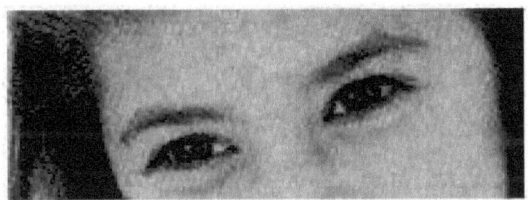

Admittedly, it is difficult to see the lines at the corners of her eyes, but look beneath the eyes. Those lines spreading out beneath her eyes are "smile lines" not wrinkles of the aged.

And what about this happy hockey player?

You can barely make out the lines under the visor that protect his eyes. But who could argue with the happiness of that partly toothless smile?

And finally, another smile of joy. Note in this picture how the actual smile zone fills an area in the center of the face.

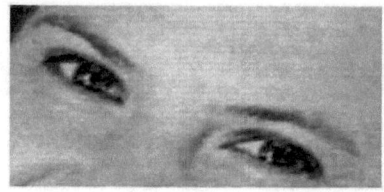

The point is – these are happy smiles and the average lay person can read them as such. Because they are happy smiles we can have fun with them and use a little humor. But now examine a different type of smile which is not really happy nor is it hostile. It is a grateful, "thank God I survived" type of smile.

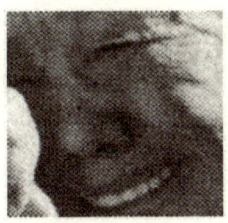

The context of this photo is the rescue of this woman from a mudslide. But does anyone really need the context to be able to decipher her feelings. The expression on her face is a smile, characterized by the stretching of her facial features. It is this stretching aspect which is the ultimate sign of a "real" smile which is a smile that is caused by some type of happiness be it a rescue from a mudslide or being elected a bishop.

What could have been the cause of the following "smile?"

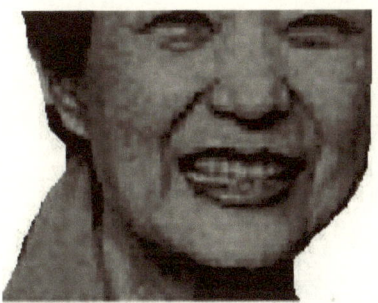

What's missing from this "smile" which removes it from the category of a happy smile? There isn't any expansion of the skin around the eyes and upper face. In fact, there is a severe tightening of this area. The only feature of this photo which suggests a smile is the mouth which does seem to be set in a type of smile.

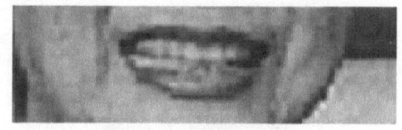

{THIS DOES LOOK LIKE A SMILE, DOESN'T IT?}

But it should more appropriately be termed a grimace. The woman pictured is in distress. There is one feature that is a direct indication of this and that is the severe crinkling of her nose. This activity is linked to the emotion of disgust or loathing. What's so intriguing about this photo is that the subject has managed to combine the two completely opposite emotions of joy and loathing in a single expression. Try smiling happily and crinkling your nose like hers.

There isn't any mistaking what a crinkled nose like this means in facial language:

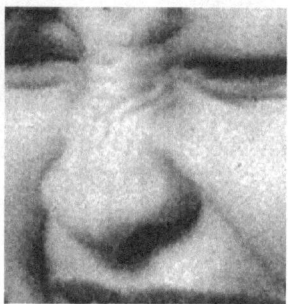

DISGUST

Why is this woman pretending to smile? Probably to cover up her true feeling of disgust. This woman was in a threatening position in which she would have been punished if she openly revealed her true feelings.

Look just a little bit closer at this photo. Note the extreme tightening of the eyes. Not a soft closing but a firm, hard eyelid shut type of closing.

She looks like she's in pain. There's a reason that these sets of photos are being focused on so closely and this has to do with *MICRO-EXPRESSIONS* which will be dealt with shortly.

Hiding displeasure behind a smile is very common. Most people have smiled to evade an embarrassing situation. In fact, people are known for smiling during periods of discomfort to avoid the discomfort. But everyone can recognize the smile for what it truly is.

To explain the various types of smiles it is important to know the origin of the smile. Like the handshake, the beginnings of the smile were not innocent. It comes from our distant past and is a shared feature with our primate relatives, particularly the baboon. Notice the baboon below.

He isn't yawning in the sense that humans yawn and he isn't howling. He really isn't smiling either but it's from this expression that the smile developed from one of our earlier hominid ancestors. The pictured baboon is making a facial gesture which says to another baboon, "I am subordinate and I will not challenge you." Over the millions of years this feature was refined into a smile by human beings, but it says the same thing as does the baboon. "Don't worry, I'm friendly." By its very nature, the smile is either a welcoming expression or meant to assure the other person or to protect the person doing the smiling.

People are attracted to smiles. In general, people can naturally decipher a smile that is not a happy smile but one that is being shown for a variety of other reasons. Research has found that it is almost impossible to produce a true smile when you are sad. Take the test. See what type of smile you produce when you think about something that makes you feel bad. Or, if you must convince someone you are happy to see him, think about a very happy time in your life just before you are to meet this person. Bring this happy moment to mind as you greet him. Is this deception? Yes. Will he decode it? Probably.

Smiling can make a person feel good. A smile releases endorphins into the system which are the chemicals that cause happiness. Smile long enough and you may get happy. Of course, this can also be overdone.

Because smiling makes people feel good, they feel good when another person smiles at them. This type of smile exchange creates a type of positive bond between two people, assuming that the smiles are genuine.

The smile below is the type most people would like to see.

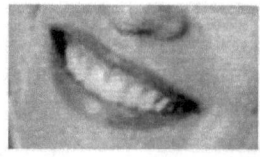

But not just because of the mouth, remember. When evaluating facial or body language it is critical that you get "corroborating evidence" of the true emotion being shown. With a smile – match the expression of the eyes that accompany the configuration of the mouth.

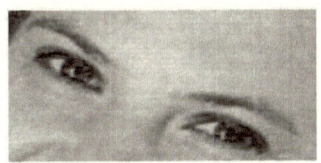

The upper pair of eyes are really happy eyes. They are wide with pleasant excitement. Ask yourself: have you ever experienced a genuine smile from someone peering at you through eyes pressed almost closed like those below?

Also pay attention to tilt of the head. The woman whose pleasant smile has just been noted had her head decidedly tilted to the left. In this case it's a sign of genuine interest. A head tilt is usually good and seldom negative. More on that later.

As a rule, smiles are not that difficult to translate. The main focus in deciphering them is the area around the eyes. If that facial area is expansive and showing lines in the skin radiating outward from the corners of the eyes it is most likely that the smile is a genuinely happy one. Don't be fooled by the mouth and the lips. That's where the forced and faked smile is made. The mouth may look happy but look to the eyes for the true emotion being expressed.

When the smile is mentioned and note is made about how a true smile can be read in the eyes, this does not imply the eyeballs themselves. Some people may be confused by this. Behind the eyeballs is where a person's inner self resides not in the eyeballs themselves. So, when it is stated that the nature of a smile is determined by the eyes, this does not mean these:

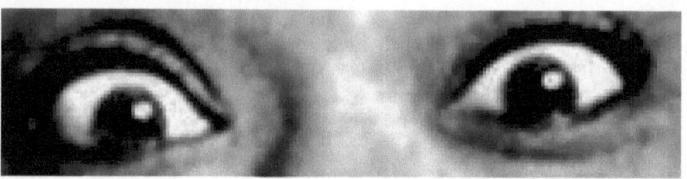

Again, what is being referred to are the lines that radiate outward from the sides of the eyes and below the eyes. This part of the exterior visual system is unconsciously controlled by a muscle called the Orbicularis Oculi.

Orbicularis Oculi.

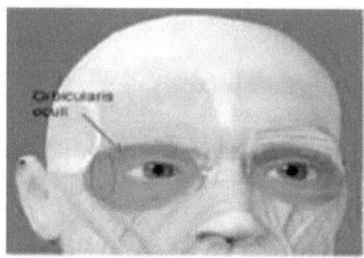

That's what produces the REAL smiles.

The mouth of course is a part of the smile but usually not the most significant part as noted. However, there are exceptions. But before examining one of them, try another test. Can you smile with your eyes when your mouth is down-turned into a frown?

It cannot be done.

Although some people still try.

There are all kinds of smiles. How many of them do you use? And do you know what messages you are sending the observer?

Let's look at the overjoyed smile. It involves the mouth in an important way and is one of the few times in which the mouth does have a primary role in a smile. And in this case, it involves the muscle called the *Orbicularis Oris* which is along the edge of the mouth on both sides.

The overjoyed smile takes the truly happy smile to its fullest possibility with the help of the *Orbicularis Oris*. You simply cannot contain your joy. And you show it by extending the muscles of your mouth to an even wider degree than you probably ever considered. It is the one case where the mouth IS as important as the eyes.

Try this mental test on yourself. You are looking in your clothes drawer for a piece of paper of some type. While searching, you locate a twenty dollar bill you did not know you had and might smile like this:

However, when you check further, you locate a lottery ticket. When you check it against the winning numbers, you discover that you've just won 10 million dollars. Then you might burst out with an overjoyed smile, like:

Notice the two things different from a common everyday smile. Firstly, the eyes are closed like the person who is happily surprised. But this is more than only being happily surprised; it is being overjoyed! This causes a natural secondary widening of the mouth at the corners. It's a widening that can actually be felt...and even heard. Consider the expression "cracking a smile."

When this secondary stretching of the mouth muscles occurs it can be felt if a person is paying attention to it (which most people aren't). And it feels good. Think of how a good, full, wide stretch of your arms feels. Same thing here but with your mouth.

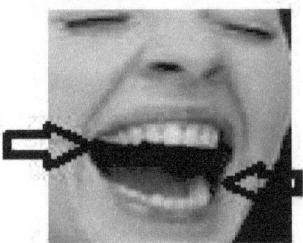

Think of this the next time you break into a super wide smile. There is also another action that many women (seldom males) add to this hyper smile. They press their hands alongside of their cheeks

The reason for this seems to be one of containment. A way to keep the emotions from becoming too overpowering. This as yet is speculation since there hasn't been a lot of research done on this particular behavior.

However, it is also a smile that is so extreme that it is almost painful. Again, look toward that spot between the eyes at the bridge of the nose. Here an important rule is broken during the display of an overjoyed smile. What would normally be considered a sign of pain is just the opposite in this specific case.

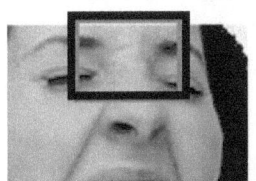

But not the same as this below because the rest of his so-called smile is not genuine:

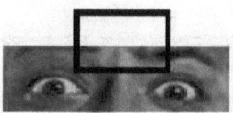

And if you're a guy, your overjoyed reaction to something is pretty much the same, with the exception of hands not being raised to the face.

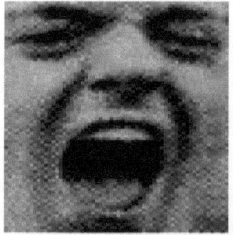

Eyes are closed and mouth is as wide as it can get. For men, this can usually be seen at a sporting event of one kind or another. Why don't men throw their hands up to their faces? Probably because men are less likely to be inhibited when expressing these types of feelings than women. Try to get a man to cry and here you will find deep inhibitions.

It's hard to misinterpret the meaning of an expression like the ones above. It might be a good time to ask someone in this frame of mind for that favor you've been wanting for awhile. And, on the flip side, if you're the one with the super wide smile, you might prepare yourself for others to approach you in search of favors. This kind of a smile attracts people to you quicker than the normal variety of smile.

This is just one way how learning to analyze your own signals can be of great benefit to you in understanding those of others.

There's also one vital feature to look for which sometimes accompanies a smile. It's called the **"eyebrow flash."** It's when the eyebrows rise instantly but not detectably because it's such a rapid movement.

Photographs of this action are incredibly difficult to obtain because the eyebrow flash is a *micro-micro-expression.* It happens so fast that you only recognize it subconsciously. But it is one of **THE MOST POWERFUL** of all signals a person will send.

Have you ever met a person for the first time and felt an immense attraction to that person but did not know why? It may be because this person offered you an **"eyebrow flash"** upon introduction. It is so important because what the **"eyebrow flash"** says is: "Wow, you are really someone very special!" The person who offers you this expression probably doesn't even know she did. But she would know subconsciously that she meant to send it. Something about you had really impressed her on sight!

The **"eyebrow flash"** shouldn't be confused with the basic raising of the eyebrows which you will be able to detect. Normally raised eyebrow are usually a form of surprise. The longer the eyebrows remained raised, the bigger the surprise. Only the context will be able to define whether it is a happy surprise or not.

Other eyebrow activity to be noted are the lowered eyebrows. This means that the person is in disagreement with you and doesn't really want to hear any more of what you're saying. Like in the photo below:

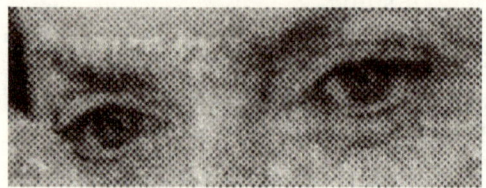

This is an action photo and was very difficult to obtain because, similar to an "eyebrow flash," this type of gesture is quickly made. The woman in the above picture had been arguing with her adult daughter and had come to a point where she wasn't interested in hearing any more. I knew the context and got the photo.

Reading the Full Face

The eyes of course are a main feature – probably THE main feature – of the face and their positioning reveals a great deal about what a person is feeling and thinking. This is well known information but it can also be very tricky when variables are added. Beginning with these eyes, what do they say?

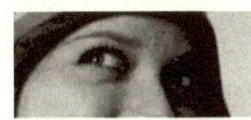

She is clearly glancing up to **her** right. This may imply that she is using the part of her brain that centers on memory. What does this tell us? That she is being truthful in her thoughts because she is tapping into her real memory area to respond to you. But what if…?

And looking upward to the left is supposed to denote something else entirely. This has been called a sign of deceit. The reason being that the mind is supposedly trying to draw an answer from the creative part of the brain in order to come up with a personally beneficial response. But consider the following.

It matters if the person is left or right handed. Theoretically it must. The basic concept is that the left handed person and right handed person are controlled by opposite sides of the brain. Thus, if a right handed person looks to the right he is being truthful by bringing up thoughts from memory. But if a left hander peers to the left she is being deceitful by bringing up the imaginative part of the brain to make up something to say even though it may be more natural for her to look to the left. That's one reason why I do not accept this theory of judging a person's honesty by which direction his eyes are turned.

There are too many confusing variations for detecting the truth by eye movement to be useful. I disavow the accepted concept because it is too unsure to be useful and has never been proved to be correct!

What if the person being tested by eye movement is ambidextrous? Which side of the brain is directing movement of the eyes?

Add to this the chaos that contradictory body language can create. For example, what if the person is looking up to the right (a supposedly truthful pose) but keeps his arms folded tightly to the chest, meaning not entirely communicative. Add to this the fact that his feet are turned away from you and are pointing away as if in escape mode? All signals indicate that this person is not being totally honest with you.

The point being made is that the belief that a person's honesty can be determined by which direction his eyes are directed is fallacious and not supported by the evidence.

Continuing with the eyes: what message does blinking send? Generally speaking, a person who blinks a lot is a person in stress who might be lying to you. One exception to this is if she has dilated (enlarged) pupils and is looking somewhat fixedly at you while blinking often. This implies romantic interest or intoxication, or both. This is the only time that a person's eyes should be dilated in normal lighting unless they are heavily drugged. It is normal for eyes to dilate in the dark.

The overall way that a person gazes at you is extremely important. If someone is peering hard and uninterrupted at you – and his pupils are contracted (small) – this is a sign of potential attack. This will be studied later in the book, but it is a clear sign of hostile intent. Most people are instantly made uncomfortable by such attention but may not be aware of how dangerous such an expression is. A person who simply doesn't like you will not fix a steady gaze upon you. A psychopath who wants to harm you will. This type of person has no fear and his intent is to terrify you. Do not give this type of person a moment of your time. Depart quickly.

Similarly, a person who absolutely will not look at you directly in the face is also suffering from some form of anti-social problem. This refers to someone who has a fixed gaze somewhere off in the distance and doesn't really acknowledge you. While he may not be personally threatening, this type of person may lead you into trouble.

The nose reveals more information than most people realize. One of the most obvious motions is the crinkled nose that we've already picked on.

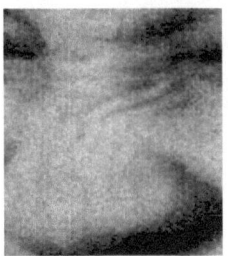

A sign of disgust. Don't let this happen to you.

Angry eyes are something we come across often. But they are so expressive that they usually do not need to be deciphered. Notice the pair below.

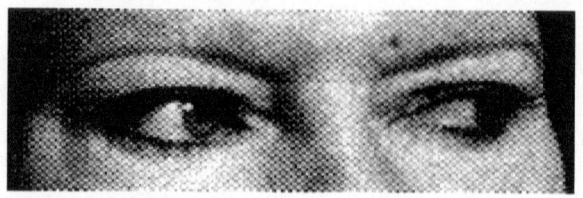

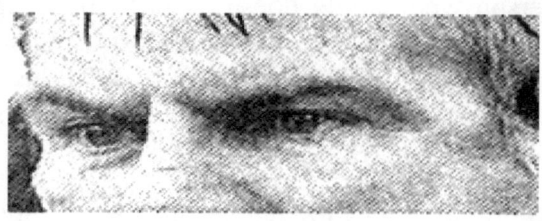

Unfortunately, movement can't be seen in these photos. However, I would not be surprised if the bottom pair of eyes are actually twitching with rage. Ironically, it is the twitching movement which would prevent these as being classified as psychopathic eyes. Why? Because the twitching implies that some form of self-control is being brought into play and the result is that the eye movement is being – with difficulty – kept in check. That's what the twitching would be doing - controlling.

While movement of the nose itself commonly occurs to send messages the nose is also often used as a signaling device.

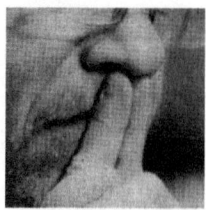

Watch out for this one. No, this man isn't double picking his nose. But he is touching it with two fingertips.

Much worse, he's doing this during a Congressional investigation. Touching the nose is considered a sign that the person is withholding information or simply lying. In this case, it might be better for this man to claim that he was only picking his nose.

The above photo is slightly different and shows an added dimension to the nose touch. Notice how the man's fingers are tightly interwoven. This implies that not only is he not going to reveal anything truthful now but he doesn't intend on doing so in the future. The investigation might just as well end right now!

There is one other very important use of the nose made by males exclusively. A slight widening of the nostrils. This display means he is sexually interested. It's a trait which makes perfect sense. It is a mainstay of our hominid past when the male would slightly open his nostrils to sample the scent of the person whom he is attracted to. This is a fact that is well known by the perfume industry.

Of course, widened nostrils aren't the same as flared nostrils when someone performs heavy breathing out of rage. This is so clearly a sign of intense anger or frustration that it doesn't need explanation.

One other point about the nose of which to be aware is the subtle twist to the right or the left made by both genders. This indicates dislike.

The chin is also commonly used as a vehicle of hidden message transmission. A chin that is resting in the hand is commonly a sign of boredom.

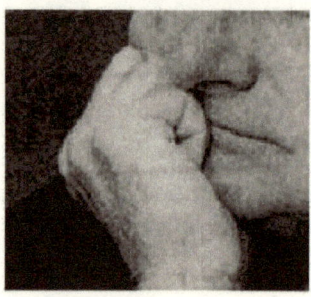

CLEARLY BORED

The woman below may seem to be smiling but she is also bored.

Watch out for the next photo. When a person strokes his chin it is usually a sign that he doesn't believe what you are telling him.

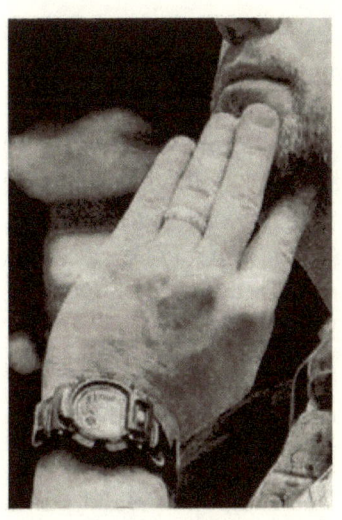

HOPE THIS ISN'T YOUR BOSS!

It's important to note the two different types of chin stroke. Shown in the one above, the man is using his **<u>fingers</u>** to do the stroking of the chin. This is different from someone who is stroking the chin with the **<u>whole hand</u>**. In the second case the stroking means that the person is interested and listening to you and not negatively judging you.

This next photo below is a really confusing one. The person is engaged in various conflicting actions all at the same time. His chin rests in his hand, declaring boredom. He is stroking his face with a forefinger, sending a message that he isn't believing what he's hearing. But the finger pretty nearly extends to the nose, meaning that he himself is hiding something. A great deal can be read from one simple action.

There's even more. The man in the above photo is doing something else as well. He is tilting his head slightly upward. A head tilted upward is commonly a sign of arrogance. And that depiction fits closely with the context in which this photo was taken where this particular individual was displaying his arrogance. Remember, part of the reason evaluations can be made is that I am aware of the context in which the photos were taken and the context in turn verifies the body and facial language.

Resuming with tilting heads. A head tilted to one side is usually a sign that the person is listening to you with interest. The picture below is a good example of this. This one is a staged photo.

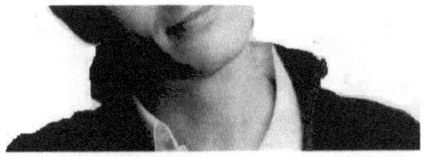

In the photo below, the woman may be listening to you, but is she bored?

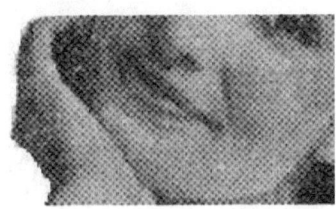

She isn't stroking her chin – which would be a sign of listening – but the chin rests in her hand which is a sign of boredom or fake interest. But her smile is genuine. It appears that she is a true friend who may be somewhat interested in what the other person is saying but not enthralled. There can be extenuating circumstances with each evaluation. Everything isn't either/or.

There isn't a lot to say about the ears. Scratching one's own ears is often a sign that this person is suffering from a lack of confidence. Reddening of ears means that someone is trying to deceive you. So, if you should come across someone who is scratching big red ears you might be leery of what he is telling you. The ears become red as a biological reaction to stress.

And, of course, always beware of a person like the one pictured below.

    Above is an ad theoretically showing a man who is angry and frustrated beyond containment. But did they get the facial language right? Specifically – the mouth? Is that the mouth of a man who is angry and frustrated beyond containment?

    Take a quick test based on the features of the man in the photo above. Did they choose the right type of mouth, or should they have chosen from one of those below? Should they have picked...

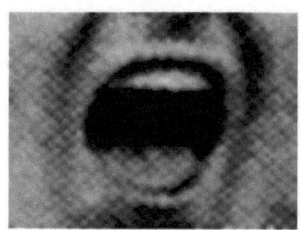

A

B

Or...

C

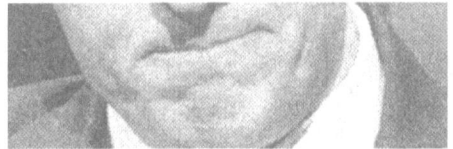

to show the type of mouth belonging to a man frustrated beyond control?

Let's see. Below...

Mouth A is of a man who is very happy and smiling so widely his mouth is wide.

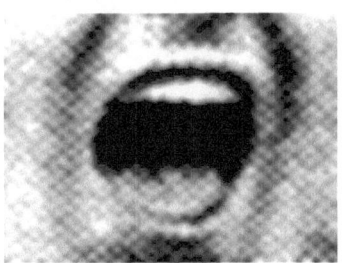

Mouth B is of a man with puckered lips. This feature usually represents a person having a bad recollection about something – a sour experience.

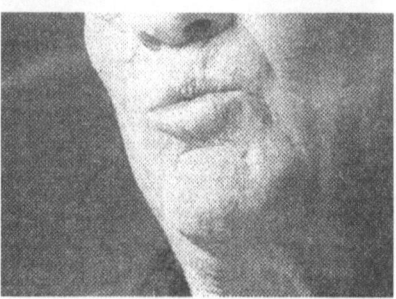

Mouth C is of a person discussing an economy in crisis. Tight lips are a sign of extreme anxiety and worry.

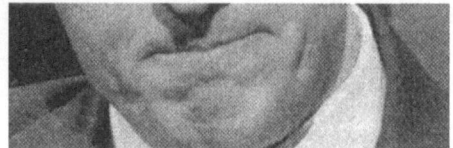

Below is what the faces based on these types of mouths would look like. Which of these truly represent an

angry/frustrated man beyond containment?

A?

B?

C?

The bottom face - C - would be correct, using mouth C.

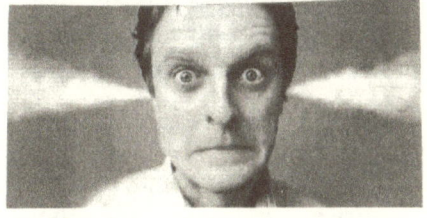

Anger and frustration beyond containment.

Body Language Self Defense

There are many ways that one person tries to intimidate another person with non-verbal behavior. He might tower over another person and peer threateningly upon him. He might severely cross his arms in front of the intended victim and scowl horribly. She may pace slowly back and forth behind someone to make him uneasy. Or even a handshake may be used to intimidate. A handshake?

What follows is what I call the <u>HANDSHAKE EQUALIZER</u>. You have probably experienced this. A person – either male or female – approaches you and forcefully extends a hand in seeming greeting.

(Schoolboard meeting, Sandusky, Ohio)

You accept the so-called friendly greeting but much to your surprise – and pain – the other person clamps your hand into a vice type grip and vigorously pumps your arm while staring over the top of your head. This person doesn't really want to shake your hand but he does want to overpower and humiliate you to demonstrate his power over you.

Most people are overwhelmed by this activity and the only thought that comes to mind is to simply outlast the handshake and let the perpetrator go away and pursue another victim. But he is a bully and it might be useful – both for your own self esteem and that of others – to counter his "attack." And this can easily be done without resorting to a true physical confrontation.

Here is one of the very best ways to deter the hand crusher. Grasp his, or in this next case her, elbow with your free hand. This symbolically and physically takes away the force of her grip. Yes, women can bully men.

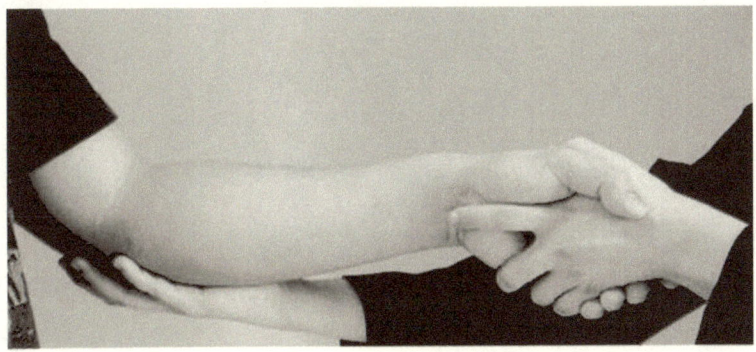

In the above photo, you would be the person on the right who has brilliantly slipped your hand beneath the elbow of your handshaking assailant. Now, at this point, he or she may even counter your move by putting an even stronger grip upon your forearm just above the wrist.

The man on the left in the picture below has the person on the right in his clutches. Would you really call this a handshake?

And there is a way to counter this. You may counter this move by pressing your free hand down upon the other's shoulder or possibly even grab him by the upper arm.

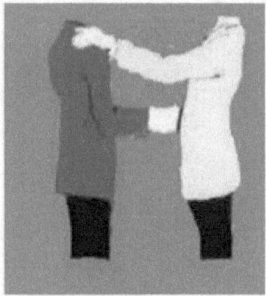

OR

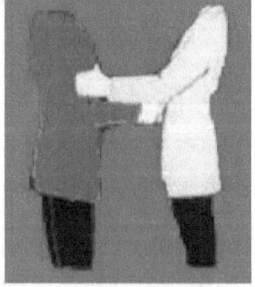

He then can even counter your counter move. This of course could go on for quite a while. But you probably will have the common sense needed to end the game and release yourself from this idiot and be happy you held your ground.

And holding your ground is something else you may literally have to do when confronted by a body language aggressor. Another one of their primary tactics is to ignore the commonly accepted rules of personal space – roughly six to ten inches in a social setting – and lay claim to as much space as he or she desires.

One method of doing this is simply by spreading themselves out as broadly as possible and literally taking up space. This is a common activity of many men in public who force the weaker and smaller in society – not limited to short women but smaller men and children as well – to make less room for others while they command more room for themselves. The following example should be viewed as an extreme case and may not necessarily be preventable.

Suppose you found a man hogging space on a commuter train:

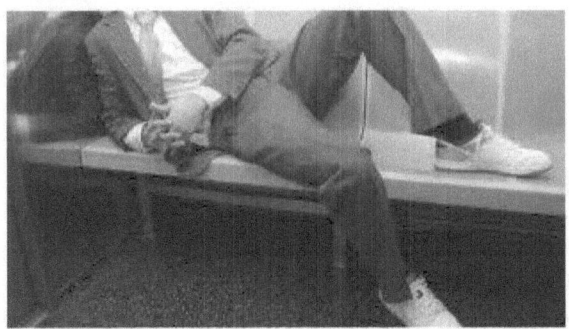

What to do in this situation? Most people would ignore it and allow the jerk to take up most of the seat. But there are ways to deal with this problem.

One remedy would be to squeeze into the tiny area that has been left for occupancy and proceed to expand your area by placing objects between yourself and the space hog beside you. You may be surprised by how this type of person reacts when his own personal space is being threatened. His naturally cowardly self may come to the fore and cause him to shrivel into a smaller space.

Of course, this would only be successful in an ideal situation where you are not in any real danger from the other person whose behavior is basically loutish rather than psychotic. It isn't worth risking your safety over a seat on a train, subway or bus. But in nonthreatening situations, keep in mind the concept of building a wall of objects to separate yourself from the lout in question and thereby increase your own stretching room.

But what if your hands are empty and you have nothing to place between yourself and the space hog after you squeezed into that tiny space? You can use the power of your vision. Stare at the area at his feet where there still remains that free space. But do it somewhat politely. Remember, you aren't the bully. But you would like to assert your rights.

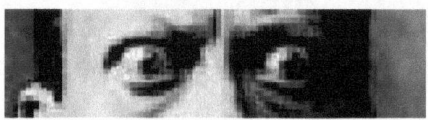

If the space hog has any sense of decency he will allocate a little more room to you. But he may be a man without conscience. In this case, you may have to settle for the territory you have won. As you know, it isn't a perfect world and sometimes the only way to defeat a social aggressor is by drastic measures which for our purposes are not the best choice.

Body language bullies use all types of techniques in social situations to intimidate others. One of the most common is the stare down – highlighting the word DOWN. This is because the perpetrator places himself in a position where he is literally peering downward at his "victim." A former American president was particularly adept at this.

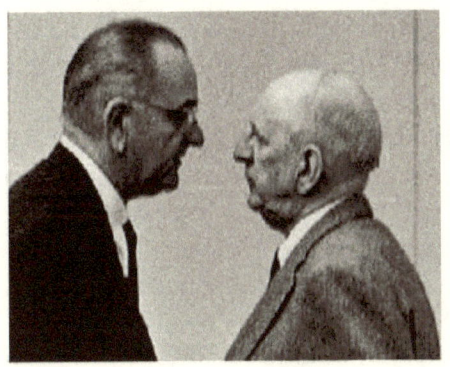

In the above photo, LBJ is performing three acts of intimidation at the same time and severely applying the pressure. He is staring at the other person, he is staring downward at him and he is closely encroaching upon his personal space. What would you do in such a situation, assuming that it wasn't LBJ who you were facing? Do you think you are hopelessly trapped? Not so. There is a way out by using your own body language to counter the assailant's.

You could have done this to LBJ. Immediately give yourself access to a great deal more space by doing the following:

Putting your hands on your hips with your elbows spread wide gains you a lot more space in any situation. Especially when you twist to and fro a little bit. Try it. It also makes you feel better. Just don't overdo it.

But how do you deal with the issue of being stared at from above if the other person is simply taller than you? One of the best tactics is movement. Look around **purposefully** from side to side, pick up a drink from a nearby table or perform some other action which takes the pressure off of you. In this way you have defeated the other person's staring and eliminated his height superiority.

Another action to take is to raise yourself to a higher level by stepping up on any available nearby object. Is there a stepstool nearby?

Maybe even a flight of stairs? A small ladder? Consider the options. The idea is to make yourself higher than the lout who is harassing you.

Of course, there is a very simple way of dealing with someone who is giving you the staredown:

However, as developed by Larry and Shemp and Curley of the Three Stooges, there is a counter tactic the other party could use. The block.

{The author is not seriously recommending poking people in the eyes.}

Some body language aggressors choose not to look you in the eye on purpose. They do this so as to belittle you. You are so insignificant that you do not rate their full attention. How do you deal with this situation? Putting aside the idea that this is not the type of person with whom you want to associate anyway it is useful to know how to counter this form of deviant behavior.

There are numerous ways to force at least a short period of eye contact. One of my favorites is this:

CLAP

A short, sharp clap. That generally draws attention quickly. Once you have the inconsiderate boor's attention you can politely excuse yourself and make contact with other more agreeable people.

Some forms of body language can reach serious and threatening levels. There are some people who will extend their reach so far as to acquire not only your space but your possessions and even you yourself by the use of touch and manipulation.

The harassment may seem to begin simply enough with the other person grabbing onto the back of your chair.

It then escalates to his tampering with your paperwork:

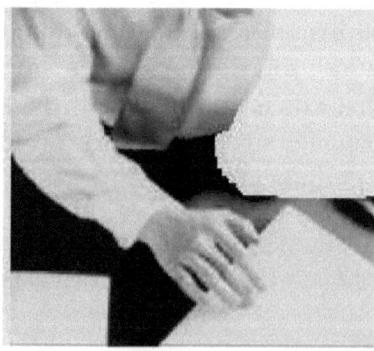

Next he will take control of your keyboard:

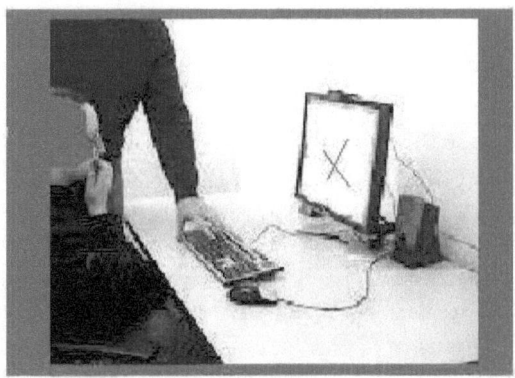

And then he will focus on you:

You unfortunately may know all about this type of behavior. If is performed by your boss a special type of problem exists which hopefully can be handled through labor laws (if they still existence as of this writing). If it is performed by someone of a lower hierarchical level whose sole purpose is to bully and dominate you then other solutions are possible.

It must be stopped from the beginning. Like all bullies – he will not quit with his initial attempts at humiliation. You also are probably very familiar with the steps about to be suggested for ridding yourself of this pest but a refresher never hurts.

The first thing to be done is remove the papers from the grasp of the other person. Do not worry about insulting him; he is insulting you. This immediately sets the no nonsense tone of your reactions.

When he tries to command the keyboard you counter the move by drawing your chair fully in front of your work area and assuming complete control of the keys and thereby forcing him off. It is also useful to spread your elbows widely to the sides of you.

There are a number of ways to react when the other person places a hand on your shoulder but the least confrontational would be to simply reach for a nearby telephone – automatically freeing yourself of his hold – and by next making a cryptic announcement to the effect, "I need to contact my supervisor." Don't say why. If a telephone is not available, reach down for some other common desk top object whether or not you need it. But do start using it anyway.

Of course, you could reach down for the pepper spray in your desk drawer, but this would probably be too provocative. Reaching farther down into a lower drawer for some object would be effective. At this point, the social aggressor may reach downward for you. That's the time for a sudden pushing backward of your chair if it is on wheels or ejecting yourself from it if it has none.

Meeting Strangers

This is one of the most common things that occurs in public – meeting strangers. And it is often the most stressful of situations for many people. Hopefully, the following information will help. A realistic example will be used for illustration purposes.

Picture yourself entering a room full of people. Assume that they are all strangers who are there to discuss the city's plan to lengthen the sidewalk alongside a street on which you live. What is going to follow is basic body language interpretation, focusing on an everyday event.

Why have you been brought to this meeting you may ask? Why the fiction? Simple really. It would be pretty boring for you to simply view a group of photos and have explanations beside them as to what they signify.

A meeting is an excellent place to view and interpret body and facial language. Also, these photos are of people who actually are going to and participating in a meeting! These are not staged so the reactions you will be seeing are real. And there are all types of people at meetings like this, including bullies and otherwise obnoxious people so the topic of dealing with them will be part of the scenario.

Begin with an individual's entrance into the meeting room. How about this entrance?

No, he's probably in the wrong room because all the lights are off and it's empty. Try the next door.

One of the primary features of your physical entrance is presenting a posture that is erect – not slumping – with a head that is held in a level position.

Below is a lilting, twisting, "look at me" type of entrance. What would you think of this type of entrance into a roomful of strangers? Seems friendly but a little...too giddy maybe.

Note the movement of the woman's body in the entrace just witnessed. All that twisting is confusing to the viewer. Which way is she going? Is she trying to avoid me or approach me?

The next entrance is a little different.

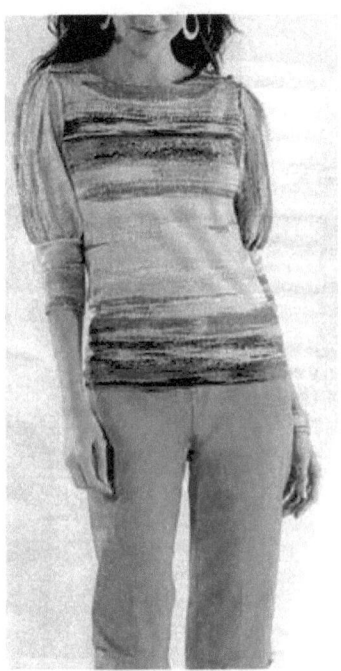

She seems composed and quite natural. The hands at the sides (not directly in front of her) reveal calm assurance. Her downward held tilt might cause some problem though because it borders on the flirtatious.

Another entrace at another time looked like this:

In an ordinary situation it's a stance that is saying, "Here I am. And I won't be easily chased off." Ever try running with hands on hips and elbows protruding? Yes, this actually is what the non-verbal signal is: "See, I'm here and I'm not going to be run off." But this is more of a show of confidence than a challenge and would be seen by an intimidator as a sign to stay away.

A male's entrance with hands on hips would be expected to appear somewhat different but the concept is the same.

Hands on hips mean the same thing for male and female. It is an overall friendly but showy appearance and has the same negative effect on social aggressors. Not only that, confident people are usually not a target.

Next is a common entrance these days (iphone ear).

He is entering the room – at an actual meeting of the type being portrayed now – with Iphone to ear. The trouble is he seems to be speaking loudly and there's usually a sign outside the door requesting that all devices be turned off. This is another type of bully. Loud, obnoxious, and one who has little concern for the privacy of others.

How to deal with this? One way is for another person to pull out his device in the man's sight and non-accusatorily mirror his activity, minus the shouting. The message might be understood. If several people join in, the message might be relayed even better. Or someone could show him the "turn off all devices" sign.

What to make of this body language in the next entrance?

It is clearly noncommittal. Note that one hand is in a pocket and the other is dangling free. This is a mixture of opposites. A hand buried in the pocket implies a person not open to discussion while a hand dangling freely at the side says just the opposite. This type of stance is primarily male.

Note the group of women below.

Only one out of nine women will stand with a single hand in her pocket (white circle). However, her other hand can't be seen in this photo. But it probably isn't in her other pocket.

There's something else about their hands that is very noticeable. Compare the picture of the women above with the picture of the men below:

Six out of seven men when in a line stand with their hands held in front of themselves at the front belt buckle area. Of course, I'm exaggerating the results of this one photo but the general fact is true. It's a gender based difference. Females are less "worried" about touching one another so in a group like the one above with the women in line they will let their hands dangle loosely next to each other. Men in general do not want to be seen touching other men – at least hand to hand. It's too much like holding hands. One safe place to hide them is a pocket. Another safe place is folded above the belt buckle.

Con Artists

A portion of this book was meant to deal with self analysis through body language. Often we aren't sure of our own intentions or our own true feelings when interacting with other people. But sometimes other people – who do not have our best interests in mind – can read our true feelings and use this knowledge against us.

Some of these people are who make up the class of what are called "con artists." They use the knowledge of how we are feeling based on our body language against us. While at the same time they project body language known to be "honest" so that we trust them. These people are highly skilled.

It is important to remember that most of the facial and body language presented throughout this work applies to either gender of any age. It is learned very early in life and much of it is based on biological factors. It will apply equally to a person's children as it will to the same person's grandparents.

It is very important to know how to decipher one's own body language when dealing with the assaults waged by bullies or con artists. As noted, these types of individuals prey on perceived weaknesses and seem to instinctively know how to read certain aspects of body language which make a person vulnerable to being a victim.

What is about to be presented are clues to basic body language which can make a person vulnerable to attack. A con artist who learns the types of body language a person uses when under stress can use this body language knowledge against him. It's one way con artists assault their victims. But it is just as true that if this type of stress produced body language is understood by the intended victim she can counter the body language she is revealing that is caused by this stress.

If a person is made uneasy, how is it revealed in his body language? That is the primary question at this point. If you are uneasy about something, what physical effect is it having on you? For example, what if you are deceiving a friend and feel uncomfortable about doing so? How is that discomfort expressed?

One of the most important indicators of uneasiness is found in that length of cartilage that lies between a person's eyes - commonly known as the nose. It can barely make any movement on its own. But its prime position in the middle of the face makes it an outstanding feature. A physiological aspect of the nose makes it a major gauge of truthfulness. It's a physiology that most people seem to be subconsciously aware of. And, no, it doesn't involve the nose growing in length like Pinnochio's when a person is being dishonest.

Has your nose possibly betrayed you in the past? Did it gave away a secret you were trying to keep? Did it reveal your true feelings to a neighbor or other person you would rather that no one knew? How did it do this?

Note the photograph below. When a person bridges the fingers over the nose in such a fashion it is meant to give the message : "Wait, let me think about that for a moment." Or, "I'm feeling really bad." That is the INTENDED message.

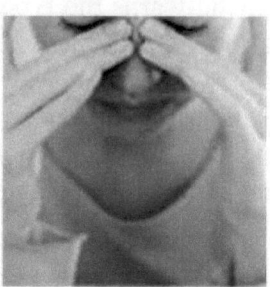

What this posture usually **really** means is: "I am deceiving you." Of course, there are the few occasions when it truly means "Wait, let me think about that for a moment," but this is not common. Bridging the fingers over the nose is a much more common clue meaning that a person is being untruthful. At this point, it is up to that person to decipher her own subconscious to determine if she is truly trying to be deceptive.

Certain devious people who are not a person's friends may be able to read the body language that admits deceit and use it to take advantage of that person - psychological blackmail. Let's focus on another non-verbal cue which essentially says, "I'm avoiding telling you the truth."

This again involves the nose, and a particular way of pinching the bridge of it:

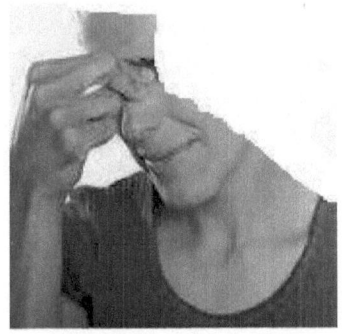

Doesn't it seem that the nose is a magnet for the fingers of someone who is hiding information? Can this be purely coincidental? Or does the nose hold some special secret that most people are only aware of on a subconscious level? "Something smells fishy!" an observer might announce in response to the hidden deception.

There is a biological reason why people in some way try to hide their noses at the same time they are trying to hide information. Even though they may not know why they're doing it.

The biology is this: when a person is hiding information the nose often turns a slight shade of red (as do the ears). For people of color the nose turns an ashen shade. In order to hide this color change a person uses the most available means at his disposal: the fingers. Some people will use a piece of tissue or other small object instead. And some are even more creative.

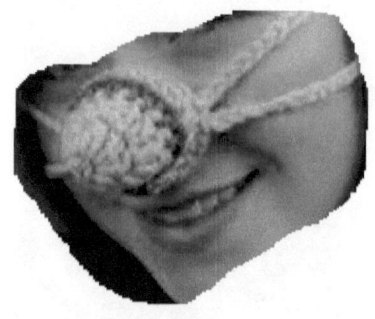

The method of hiding the discoloration of the nose is not something immediately understood on the conscious level. It is generated by the subconscious. Most people are completely unaware of what they are doing and the biological nature behind it. This was the secret method mentioned earlier about how a person can definitely determine if she herself is being untruthful even if trying to fool herself: has the skin color changed at the point where it is being hidden from view.

Considering the "con artist" again: he knows about all of these signs of deceit. And he is very careful to use NONE of them while playing a con. He knows that subconsciously most people are aware that these forms of body language are signs of deception. So he specifically refrains from using them! Most "con artists" are far from being stupid.

Have you ever found yourself using these tactics for evading the truth? The purpose of this chapter is to bring this type of information to one's attention so as to understand how it can make a person vulnerable to attack. If a person uses any of these methods – potentially for evading the complete truth – he can recognize this and question himself as to if he is not being completely truthful in a particular situation. And if not – why not. And if it is a truly important situation can some unscrupulous person take advantage of it.

There are two other very common cues that are used in truth evasion. One is the ear tug or ear scratch.

The other is when the back of the neck is scratched as kindly demonstrated by our canine friend:

Both of these methods are also performed to hide a discoloration of the skin caused by a nervous reaction to being untruthful.

There are other less direct methods used to keep from telling the truth: putting up a barrier so one does not have to answer any questions is one of these. Note the following photograph and ask yourself how does this type of physical position make you feel about the person who is using it. What does it tell you?

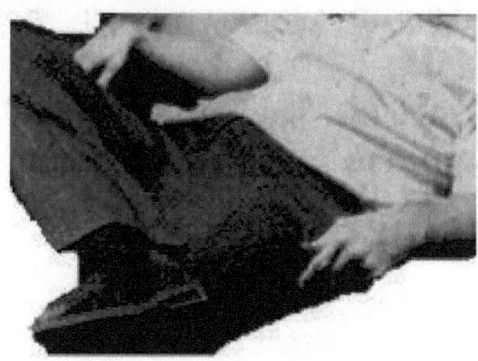

The posture of the man sitting easily back in his chair with his hands grasping the arms with his leg crossed over the knee is meant to ward off any would-be questioners. This is a person who does not want to get into any involved discussions. What is he hiding? This man may think he is safe, but someone of a more powerful and unkind nature may be able to break through his wall.

The person in the next picture is also avoiding something. He is basically saying by his gesture and head tilt, "I can't (or won't) tell you anything else. I've already said all I intend to say." This is despite the upturned palms which are overidden by the deceit of the shrug.

So what should a truthful person do with his eyes when speaking to another person? Keep them open and don't try to play the game of looking in the proper direction (right or left, up or down) in which you are supposed to be looking if telling the truth. The observer will know what you're doing and probably think you're trying to "fix" your responses.

Simply look at the other person as you normally would and try not to rigidly set the eyes in a steady gaze – the old "look 'em straight in the eyes" by way of the top of the head advice. So, don't do this:

Blink once and awhile and try to look normal. But don't blink too much since that often is a sign of tension and is biologically generated. It's difficult to hide from too many blinks.Finally, remember this advice. Keep your hands away from your nose. Don't scratch you ears. And try not to scratch the back of your neck. These are the primary clues about the head and face that reveal that a person isn't being completely honest. So, as you can see, it's easier to tell the truth, so do that.

Fist, Thumb and Forearm Power

There is more than one type of fist. Most people aren't aware of this. One type of fist is primarily meant to be used to punch someone or something. Bullies of any age group or gender know this. As do their intended victims. That is why it is so commonly used to threaten people. But there are other types of fists, too, and these will be closely examined next.

THE FIST

The fist, the thumb and the forearm are responsible for some of the most potent signals being transmitted among us, aside from signals made by the face. And just a slight difference in positioning of the thumb makes a huge difference in the meaning of a fist. For example. What's

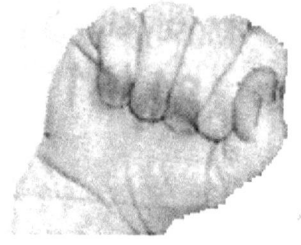

the difference between this fist:

(thumb drawn inward **beside** the fingers)

and this fist:

(thumb drawn fully **across** the fingers).

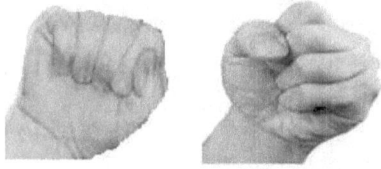

The different positioning of the thumb makes a critcal difference. The first fist showing a thumb drawn against the outside of the index finger implies a conciliatory or jubilant state of mind. Always keep careful observation of the position of the thumb. The person whose thumb is on the left above is determined about his belief but is also determined to be civil.

The thumb of the fist on the right side is firmly pressed onto the inside of the tightly drawn fingers. This implies an imminent readiness to strike. What does this tell you?

The easiest way to understand this is by simple observation. The angry fist is one that physically can be used to strike someone. As such, the thumb would not be held alongside the fingers but across the fingers. Take this test. Make a fist. Any type of fist. Would you use that type of fist to strike someone or something?

Consider actually hitting someone or something with it. If you could it would be a threatening fist because of the positioning of the thumb. Again, not all fists are threatening fists. If your thumb is held along the outside of the other fingers or is raised into an upright position this type of fist wouldn't be very effective as a striking tool.

Avoid a person whose fist is primed to strike. But what about the passive or celebratory fist? A position of strength and resolve can be demonstrated by using what I call a "passive" fist. Why even make a passive fist? The purpose of any fist is to draw attention.

A person can be adamant about an issue without becoming violent over it (or potentially violent). As noted: <u>Any type of fist is an attention getter</u>, male or female. But a threatening type of fist is certainly often used for intimidation and bullying purposes! It is only very rarely used as a celebratory gesture, but there are cases where this rule is broken. Nothing is perfect.

The type of fist you use may also provide you a way with which to accurately gauge your own true feelings on an issue. The placement of the thumb of your fist (or fists) will reveal to you the actual intensity you feel about a particular matter. Are you angry enough to threaten violence? Have you kept your thumb drawn inward and pressed down upon your fingers?

However, fists do not always signal anger. Fists thrown into the air can also signal elation. A job well done. A celebration. But these fists are always held raised in a non-threatening way.

Like this:

Her fists are directed inward toward herself. Also note the other signs this young woman is giving that demonstrates one who is overjoyed. Extra wide smile and CLOSED EYES (yes, they are). All of the language fits together like a jigsaw puzzle. But what if a non-matching piece were thrown into this picture? Let's see.

All of a sudden, her upraised arms and clenched fists give a different message. Now they seem to be a sign of frustration. Note how her arms suddenly seem completely different even though they are **EXACTLY** the same as in the other photo? It's the expression on her face alone that has changed. Almost like an optical illusion. But it isn't. The signal being sent from the position of her arms in the second photograph has changed from elation to frustration based on the expression on her face.

What about this next fist? What do you think its message is? Is it one you are likely to use?

It's a fist of threat and power used by a political leader. It is saying, "I will keep control in my hands!"

What about this next fist? What might its message be and is it one you'd use?

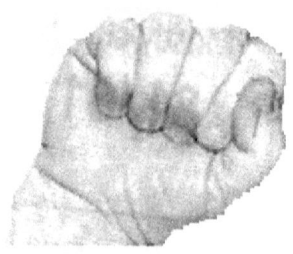

It is a fist of jubilant celebration and non threatening. Look at the two fists side by side and note the exact difference between them:

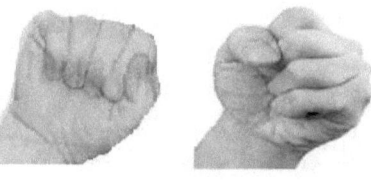

Jubilant beside angry

The peaceful fist has the thumb snuggly drawn next to the index finger. The violent fist has the thumb firmly held across the other fingers, keeping them in rigid control. The thumb controls the non-verbal message of the fist.

The ultimate point is to keep these types of fists in mind when confronting a social aggressor or obnoxious person. The type of fist he uses will show his true intention. And, you too can reflect that feeling for defense by producing the same type of fist (without the actual intent of violence). However, this is more of an escalation of hostilities than a reduction of them. The fist is basically the highest level of non-physical abuse and it is difficult to overcome other than to simply remove oneself from the situation.

THE FOREARM

Now for a part of the body that is seldom if ever considered: the forearm. First, from a non-threatening perspective. For females who are attempting to make themselves very noticeably attractive, a bare forearm is highly irresistable to a potential mate. Most women seem to know this instinctively judging by the number of bare forearms that are seen. Although, while women seem to know the attractive nature of this part of the body I don't believe that many are aware HOW powerful a lure it is.

The bare male forearm is also attractive to potential partners. But the attractive portion stops below the shoulder. For males, shoulderless shirts are generally seen as something other than attractive and have a negative association.

Again, the bare female shoulder is another matter. Show it with the knowledge that it is powerful.

Would you say that the woman on the right has a flirtatious advantage? What does your common sense and visual cue tell you? She is bare all the way to the shoulder. That gives her an edge.

And what don't you notice about the above photograph? The lack of too much ornamentation – armlets, etc. – on their arms. Ornamentation actually defeats the purpose by covering the area of flesh that a person has highlighted. The wrists are a different matter.

There are two other basic ways that the forearm is used, primarily by females. They act as either a sign of mutual accomplishment with another person – either a male or a female – or they act as a useful barrier device, either by themselves or by the forearm being given more authority when something is being held in the hand.

Her left forearm is angled across her chest while a glass of some type of liquid is held before her in her right hand. Meaning: don't get too close.

Both men and women use the forearm across the chest also as a sign of success. Something well accomplished. And that is the general conception of such a movement which you may wish to use on occasion to reveal high, but restrained, feelings of accomplishment.

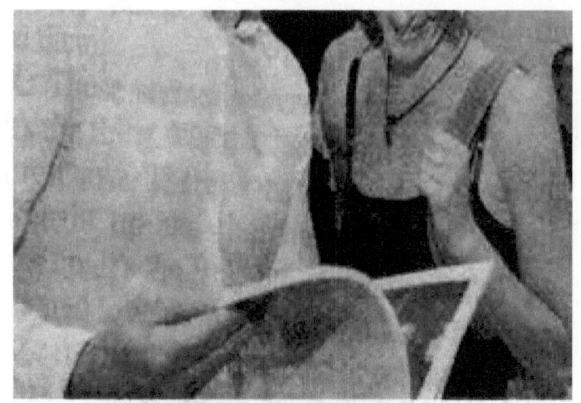

Forearms can frequently become part of a pair of crossed arms. While crossed arms are usually a sign of hostility and a desire to be left alone the interpretation can depend on over which part of the body the arms are crossed. If crossed at waist level, eagerness may be the emotion implied rather than hostility.

Use this type of crossed arms and you show a positive readiness for what lay next. A rolling up of the sleeves type of non-verbal comment.

Eagerness to get started with a project or to get a job done. The main difference is that in this case the arms are not crossed at chest level and are not making a barrier of the entire torso region.

The female version is a little different. So when you want to give the appearance of eagerness over some project or plan, this might be how you would stand if female (hands firmly clasped at waist level):

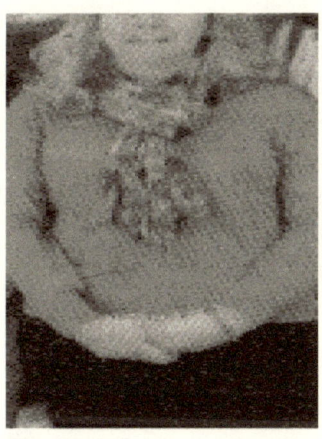

The woman above is a teacher with an exciting project she is eager to start working on.

The important difference is that your hands are clasped at waist length not a few inches lower or higher which would imply different messages to the viewer.

A quick quiz to be answered later. Note the following picture and decide which one of these three men would be the **most** likely to listen to an explanation as to why they are getting less pay now:

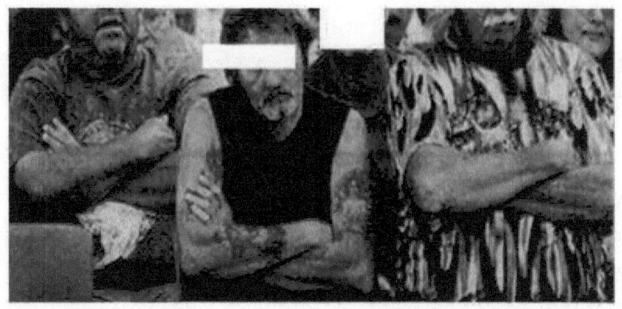

Arms crossed over the chest is one of the most powerful signs of intimidation. It is meant to intimidate, completely. Most people know the feeling of having someone stand over them with both of their arms crossed at chest level. It's the same for adults as well as children.

In some cases, the potentially intimidated person responds by also crossing his arms and standing face to face with the adversary. This is direct confrontation and puts both at the same emotional level. Who hasn't seen two children standing face to face, chin to chin, with arms folded at the chest? Adults do this, too.

Is there a better way to defuse a person standing over another person with arms folded? Yes. If the intended victim is sitting she first stands up. There is little response that can be made if remaining seated. Remember, however, these methods can only be used if the situation is a safe one and in which the other person is not a psychopath. A psychopath should never be intentionally confronted.

Once the intended victim is on her feet the best way to counter the intimidator who stands with both arms folded is to move slightly to either direction; and keep moving, slowly. This throws him completely off balance and takes away the full force of his mighty stance. In fact, in most instances, the social aggressor will not be able to maintain hold of both arms folded across the chest. Try it yourself. Fold your arms across your chest and try to move in a circular motion. In this event, the social aggressor's power literally slips away.

Another way to defeat a would-be intimidator in this situation is to raise oneself physically onto a higher level if possible as noted earlier. Looking upward at his sought after victim may loosen his folded arms.

This tactic of raising to a higher level also works when social aggressors are standing over a person in other scenarios as well.

We began this section observing thumbs and fists but have yet to consider one of the most important thumbs in history. It has often been noted and often been discussed but I have yet to see an analysis made of it. Therefore, I will do that now.

RULE OF THUMB

One of the most formidable features of human anatomy is the thumb. Some body language experts may disagree with this. My answer to them would be:

See this!

Notice the thumb. What is it doing? It is forcefully keeping the other fingers in check while at the same time presenting a formidable figure of its own.

The thumb is considered the finger that elevated humanity to the level of Homo Sapiens; the digit that allowed us to explore the totality of our creativity. The opposability of the thumb – the ability to press it with control against any of the tips of the other fingers – is critical to tool building, from the primitive stone adze to the intricate microchip.

The human subconscious is very aware of the importance of the thumb to the development of society. This is shown by the many important ways in which it is used. In ancient Rome, the thumb was used at gladiatorial events to give a ruling as to life or death of its participants. In the modern day sport of baseball the thumb is used by the all powerful umpire to render his safe or out call on the field as well as using it to eject anyone from the premises at anytime for any reason. The thumb is a handy tool for the almost lost art of hitch hiking. And the cyber world is controlled by the thumb as the primary force behind texting and is altering the functioning patterns of the brain.

Do not forget the power of thumb sucking and the effects it has had upon the developing child.

And note the power that the thumb gives to one of the most potent of hand gestures that exists:

In the U.S. and the Western World the thumbs up is a very powerful sign, a very positive sign, empowered by the might of the thumb. However, in the Mid East and that part of the world the meaning is not so positive – as I explain in my ebook "Identifying Lone Wolf Terrorists on Sight."

Some people have very successfully learned how to wield the might of the thumb. Among them are politicians.

Now for a quick quiz. Can you identify the thumb below?

It is a very important thumb indeed. It belongs to one of the foremost politicians of later 20th century.

To which of these people does the above thumb belong:

OR

One of these 2 ? Or...

Maybe?

Or…

Yes, they have all used the thumb to good advantage. But only one among those in this group has wielded astounding command of it. He is pictured below (without thumb).

Yes, the famous thumb belongs to William Jefferson Clinton. And it is not by accident that he used his thumb the way he did when making so many of his speeches. He learned the power of the thumb early in his political life and used it well. Part of the thumb's power is because it is used as a part of the fist, thus keeping attention while maintaining benevolent control. And when Bill Clinton got in real trouble there was a special trick he played with his thumb, but this will be noted momentarily.

The thumb is held firmly above the row of fingers below. His fist represents power and his dominating thumb shows his benevolent control of that power.

Also to be noted is that Bill Clinton was blessed with an exceptionally long thumb. And just as he learned to use the thumb to his advantage so too can you.

How? One way is by using it as a method of directing other peoples' attention as opposed to using any of the other fingers. For example, if you would like someone to carry out a task for you instead of pointing this way:

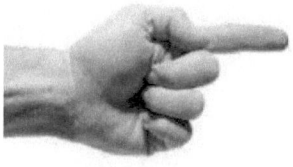

Use your thumb and point this way:

Yes, it looks awkward and you rarely see anyone pointing with a thumb. But by using the thumb as a pointer you are implying an importance about the task. You are also making any social aggressors aware that you will not be harassed by anyone.

As another example, when most people refer to themselves when speaking, don't they use their thumb to point at themselves?

A final point about hands and fingers is left to be made. Test this on yourself (if male or so disposed). Which finger is longer: your index finger or ring finger? A longer ring finger denotes a higher testosterone level. This is known because while in the womb the increased size of the ring finger is caused by a higher level of testosterone. Just out of curiosity: which finger is longer on the hand of Bill Clinton?

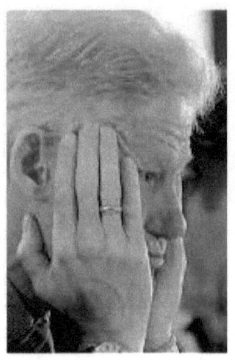

Looks like the ring finger is clearly longer than the index finger.

This would be applied in reverse for women's fingers (less testosterone = shorter ring finger). What about Hillary's in particular? Her fingers are below for comparison:

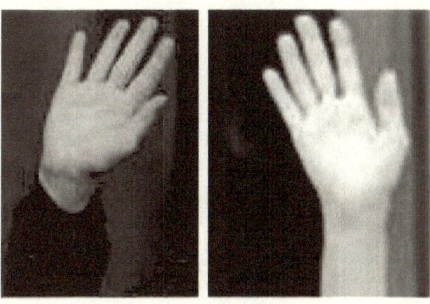

Feel free to make your own conclusions.

As noted, a fist is meant to attract attention. But look at how President Clinton expertly uses the combination of thumb and fist. The thumb is drawn in but is still pointed upward, demonstrating control. His fist represents power and his dominating thumb shows his benevolent control of that power.

A person's thumb that is hidden under the fingers represents conciliation, one that is primed firmly outside of and across the fingers shows anger. A thumb held on a slight angle above the fist (not to be confused with the thumbs up sign) suggests benevolent control of that power. And that is why President Clinton's use of his thumb in that manner while giving speeches is so important.

Now – is there a way that you can incorporate that in your non-verbal communications with others? Remember, most people will instinctively understand the message. Also remember that this type of thumb usage IS NOT the same as the common thumbs up sign. When a thumb's up gesture is made the thumb stands back from the fingers and extends noticeably above them. The Clinton thumb lays at an angle over the fingers and only peeks out above them. The signals are completely different.

Thumb's up

Thumb's peek

Of course, you have to be extremely careful how you use the Clinton thumb so that is isn't obvious or laughable. A variation of it would be best.

Back to the forearm for a moment.

Before leaving this section, the answer to the earlier quiz will be given. Here is the question again: Note the following picture and decide which one of these three men would be the most likely to listen to an explanation as to why they are getting less pay now:

The answer is – the man in the middle. Why? Because his arms are folded near his waist and not directly over his chest. What this implies is a willingness to listen to arguments. Note also the slight head tilt. This also implies willingness to listen at some level. How did you do?

Handshakes

Most people have a handshake that they almost always use to the exclusion of all others. See if the handshake you use most often is among any of those below.

There will be two sets of hands, of course, and you will need to select which of the pair you will define as yours. Do not concern yourself with the gender of the hands; look at them as if they are all androgenous. Here is the series of handshakes:

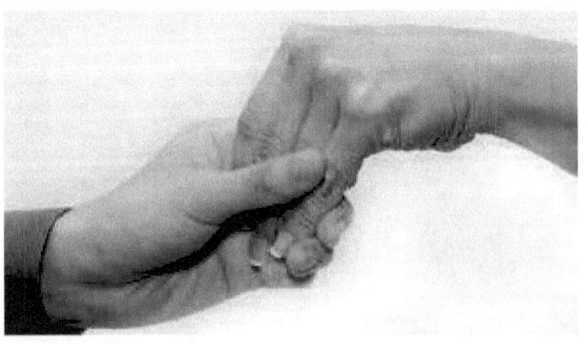

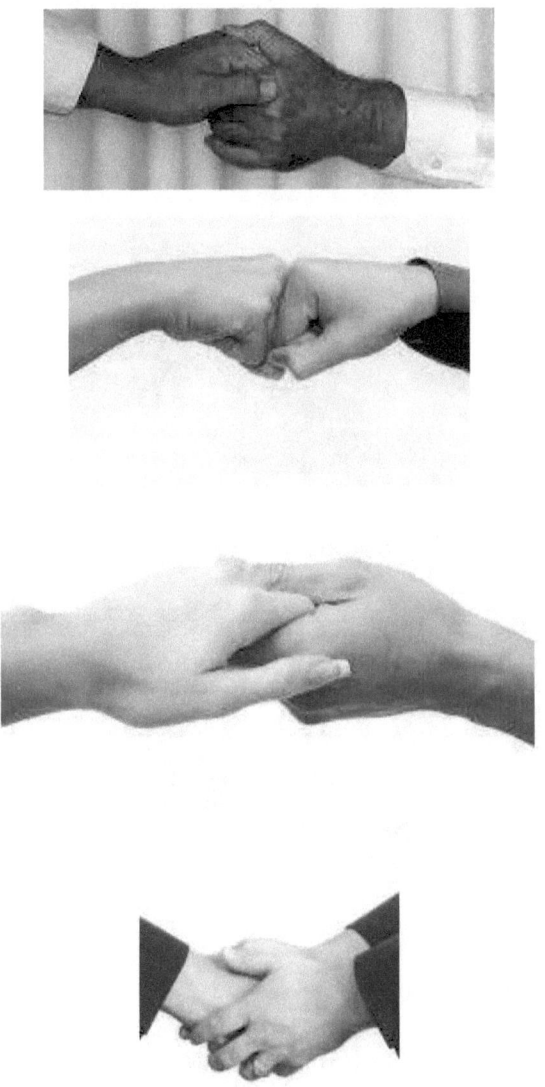

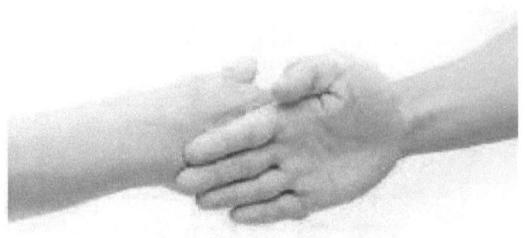

Which type of the above handshakes would you visualize yourself using? It may not even be among the ones shown above but it may fall close to one of them.

Is there a difference between a male and a female handshake? The answer to that depends on a person's point of view. In my opinion, there shouldn't be a difference. I would consider the last handshake that has been shown to be the most equal of all and either hand could belong to either gender.

Ideally, a handshake should represent either an introduction or a re-acquaintance between people. Too often it becomes a power struggle. We have already examined the ways that a body language intimidator uses the handshake. But often the "average" person attempts to use a handshake as a way to gain the upper hand, if you will.

The handshake itself defines what it means. If the hand is used as a vice it is obvious that the handshake is meant to dominate the other person with force.

If a person uses what I call a "dip" handshake, as pictured below...

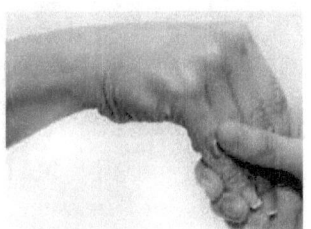

...it would seem that they are handing over, so to speak, control of the situation to the other person. Unfortunately, it is sign of weakness to a social aggressor.

Going through photographs of handshakes it becomes apparent that there is usually some form of competition occurring with one hand overpowering the other. But there are just as many handshakes where the two persons involved are simply sharing a greeting.

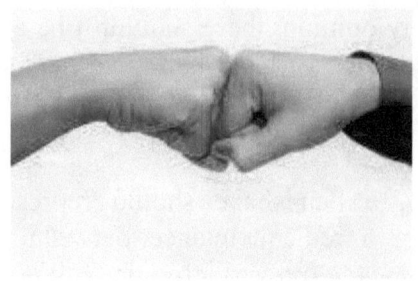

Sharing

As noted, the form of handshake that takes place will be determined by the intentions of the participants. Some handshakes are even neutral like this one:

The handshake is generally the first act that takes place after a person makes an "entrance." Often times an entrance is made into a large room where a meeting of some type is being held. The type of entrance you make should be based on the environment and your true feelings at the time. Why approach a room filled with detractors with a beaming smile? That will probably make them very suspicious. Or keep them off guard. Or – a smile being what it is – it may be the best entrance possible. In this case, it depends on the situation. The handshake may mirror the smile.

You can often control how other people view you by the non-verbal cues you send. The real secret is knowing which is the proper cue to send. And, don't worry, most people have the instinctive ability to interpret your unspoken signals. But are you sending the signals you want them to receive?

And the real point isn't to analyze just the other people at a gathering but to apply their actions to yours. Are your personal non-verbal signals the same as or similar to theirs? Do you want to be sending those particular messages? If not, you can select examples presented here and adopt them. There isn't anything negative with trying to promote a better understanding of your intended non-verbal signals.

There are many types of handshakes and many nuances to them. But have you ever seen a person take part in a handshake with himself? Watch next…

Did any of the handshakes that were reviewed look anything like the way you shake hands? If you'd like to change your style you can always do so. Just remember, a handshake is more of a competition than a simple way of introducing oneself. But if you ever find yourself being bested in a handshake and don't like it you can gain more control by using your free hand to grasp the other person on the wrist, the elbow, or alternatively by lying it over the top of both your pair of joined hands. If you haven't recognized your handshake yet, a few more follow.

Above is an interesting male to male handshake. The man on the right has attempted to gain control with a vice grip but the male hand on the left maintains equal status by spreading the fingers. It is almost certainly done subconsciously, but the man on the left instinctively knew how to maintain equality in the handshake. Have you ever tried it? Both genders can use the "finger spread" escape. Its purpose is to break the vice grip hold and keep out of the hands of a social aggressor. Below is a vice grip.

The person on the left in this photo has clearly lost this match. It is the direct opposite of the previous handshake. In this one the hand on the left is in a vice grip and the finger spread technique was not used to escape.

Below is a meeting-in-the-middle type of handshake. Truly egalitarian.

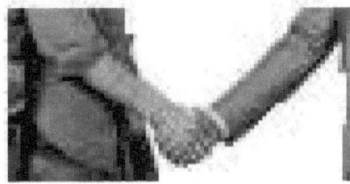

This next handshake shows total dominance by one side. The "grip and yank," I call it.

The woman on the left is completely overpowered by this handshake. Not only is her hand in a vice grip but her entire arm has been pressed back toward her body. Try not to let this happen unless you want to give the impression of being overpowered. The way to escape is simply by drawing backward from the other person.

Remember the person who tries to overpower you with a handshake. This is a sign of a social aggressor and he may act in a similar fashion on other topics. Beware. The handshake is a warning!

As you can see there are a number of handshake types but they all have a commonality to them: they are a competition which you win, lose or draw. This applies to both genders. A handshake is very similar to an arm wrestling event.

Handy Gestures

When considering non-verbal signals, the hands are among the most expressive. Also very important are the lips and mouth. A great deal of information is supplied by both. Keep in mind when viewing the following photos, the type of hand and lip movements that you yourself perform. Seek out the similarities between these photos and the signals you are sending and determine if they are the ones you intend to be sending.

Hands

Just as important as the type of signals that are being sent is how they are being interpreted by the observers. It's important to keep in mind that what you think the message your signals are sending may not be what the observers are seeing. For example, you may sit at a table with your fingers intertwined like this...

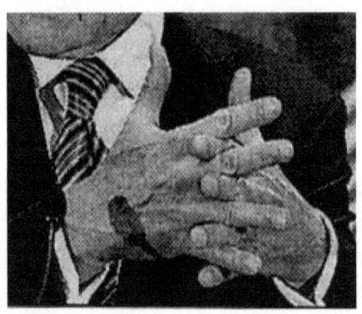

...and you may believe you are relaxed and look relaxed. But are you...really? This is a non-verbal cue which reveals that the person with twined fingers is pretty tense. Keep that in mind for yourself. Not only is this a common interpretation of entwined fingers by body language professionals it is also the professed view of psychologists and psychiatrists. This fashion of twining one's fingers denotes tension not relaxation.

So what's a better thing to do with your hands? Maybe just lay them in your lap or flat on a table top. Seems like a simple idea, but it does relieve stress. Yours and others. And things do seem to become less confused when stress is relieved, making you more composed and less of a potential victim for an intimidator or other difficult person.

Have you ever been to a meeting or seen speakers on television who have become almost violent with rage when speaking on a particular topic? This is common at political events. Below are some examples of public speakers using their hands to emphasize their points and the listeners in the audience responding with their hands.

A highly charged speaker would shout and display hand movements like this:

He is poking the air with his fingers and you can see by his face he isn't happy. Remember him? If gesturing like this continues and becomes more adamant people may

125

stop listening and begin to get very nervous. Like this person:

He is comforting himself by clasping his own hands together. We've all done this at one time or another when listening to someone who is giving an agitated speech. It gives us a sense of well-being. But it also increases our tension due to its physical nature.

This speechmaker is grabbing at the air, trying to get across a point.

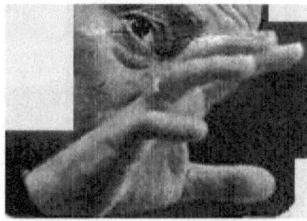

And another speaker is clawing with two hands to get her point across:

And what about the man shown next? What's the difference between him and the others who were just highlighted?

Notice the direction his hand is facing? Upward. Benevolent? Usually, except when the fingers are formed into hooks – like above. It's a general rule of the non-verbal language of hands that when the palms are facing upward the intent of the person is *usually* charitable, friendly, and helpful. But, also, when the palms are sideways or downturned – or the fingers are like hooks – the signal is generally of a negative nature.

Why? Because the positioning of the hands is reflecting the intention of the thoughts. For example, when a person tries to physically destroy something his hands are like clutching claws. Conversely, have you ever seen a peace offering presented to someone without the hands being formed into a cup or bowl shape (without hooked fingers)?

Have you ever seen anyone chasing another person in rage with his hands in the palm upward facing position? It's just a fact of nature that anger is expressed by the hands in the way that the hands are employed while in the act of violence.

If you approach with palms upward, you will often be received cordially. It's a non-threatening gesture. All hand gestures have a powerful impact on the observer.

Just as it is true that one cannot ride an acoustic guitar like a witch's broom:

Nor should you make assumptions about a dog's temperament from a distance. Note this photograph taken of a dog and his owner from the distance (taken at a bark-in-the-park day at a baseball game):

I thought that this looked like a kind of a friendly pooch who a person might want to pet and give a dog biscuit. Then I saw him up close.

I don't think I've ever seen a more terrifying looking dog! The lesson is to always look more closely at something before deciding what it really is and beware of those famous words "He won't bite." In reply to that I would say, "Maybe not, but he looks like he might kill."

Back to the hand language. Let's examine some interesting things that might be happening with hands aside from flailing about and poking the air. Note the following tactic.

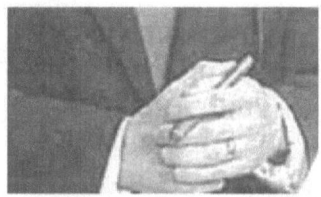

It's a use of a double barrier. First the hands are joined and placed in front the speaker and then fortified with a pen like object. This is like saying, "I'm telling my side of story but I'm not prepared to hear what you've got to say." It is a favorite device among politicians. But everyone uses this same device.

Here's another one. I call it the choke. Meant to choke off any real debate. Also popular with politicians.

These are important to know about because in ordinary public speaking – the type most people would likely be involved in – these types of gestures and evasions should be recognized for what they are. While the use of hands is very common in ordinary public speaking in positive cases they are used to emphasize words and to get a point across better, not to confuse and put up barriers.

Of course, this applies to all forms of speaking whether at a public event or at a school cafeteria. Note the degree of aggression in the hands.

Another favorite use of hands while speaking is to try to push people away or, basically, to not answer bothersome questions, by shoving them away with both hands.

Micro-expressions

Micro-expressions are directly related to the face and are one of the most potent weapons in the arsenal of deciphering the true meaning of an expression. A micro-expression is an expression which appears on the face for a mere micro-second and is almost never deciphered live. Most observers need to use slow motion photography to be able to see these expressions. Yet it is through the use of micro-expressions that people in the law enforcement field as well as lawyers, psychologists, and judges determine the sincerity of the people with whom they are dealing, assuming they are fortunate enough to be presented with a micro-expression by the subject in question.

Anyone can recognize and read micro-expressions as they occur but it is exceptionally difficult to do and requires a great amount of practice. It would be a useless tool for our purposes of instant recognition if a person had to rely on slow motion photography in order to observe a micro-expression. But in order to read micro-expressions a person must know exactly what to look for, where to look for it and to be **extremely** observant. Knowledge of facial anatomy would also be helpful.

What a micro-expression does is insert itself for a mere nanosecond on the face in the midst of the expression that the person is already showing. The micro-expression is generated by the subconscious without the person's knowledge and represents the **true** feeling that this person is experiencing.

A micro-expression most commonly occurs in the very center of the face, primarily around the eyes and mouth. And it can be very extreme in nature. It is like a random frame in a 35mm film appearing out of place amidst a whole series of unrelated frames. For example, it would be like a frame of cool lemonade appearing in the middle of a series of frames showing baboons grazing on an African plain.

On the human face, the micro-expression would be just as out of place. A person might be in the middle of making a reasoned, reposed speech when all of a sudden he would close his lips tightly for a nanosecond. This quick expression would represent his real feelings on the topic about which he is speaking. Below, he really would rather keep his mouth closed...

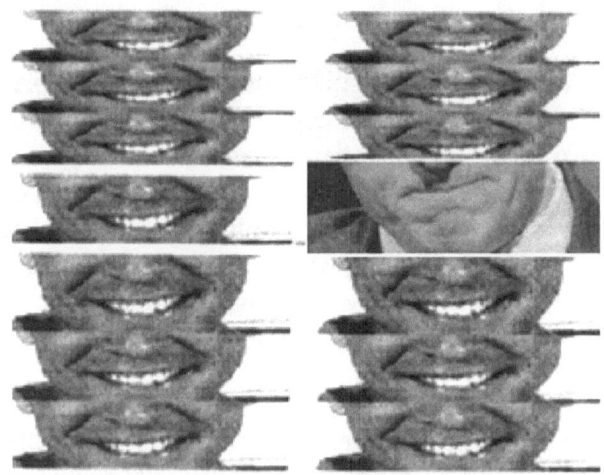

The point where the man clamps his lips together would last less than a tenth of a second and would be barely noticeable. But even if you couldn't actually see it you would be made uncomfortable at that point and not really know why. Keep that in mind. If you're in the middle of a conversation with someone or watching someone speaking and you suddenly become very uncomfortable or annoyed for no apparent reason - take note. You probably just witnessed an alarming micro-expression.

Of course, you also could get a positive feeling from seeing a micro-expression. What about the next example?

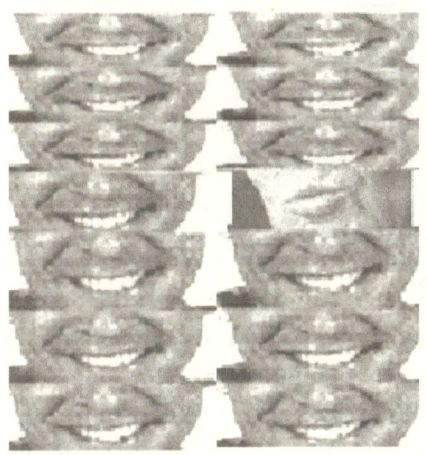

A pucker! A flirtatious movement. Something in his subconscious caused him to be flirtatious of mind. Yes, it is very common for people to flirt using micro-expressions. It's safer that way.

Below is a very common micro-expression a person could keep watch for. It's the crinkling of a nose with disgust in the middle of what seems to be an ordinary smile. The ordinary smile becomes something of a much different nature when the expression is inserted into it.

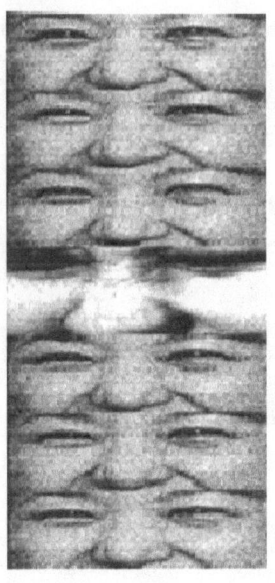

The most likely places to find micro-expressions are at the bridge of the nose, the lips, and that space between the eyebrows. These usually have negative meaning, but they must be evaluated in the context in which they occur.

A particular clue to look for in spotting a micro-expression is any type of change in color or texture of the skin (note the above examples where the micro-expressions took place). A change has occurred to the skin during the creation of the micro-expression and has affected the skin shading.

As mentioned, the study of micro-expressions isn't new but it almost always is after-the-fact. It's often done by examining slow motion footage taken of a person in question. Our task is more difficult: spotting the micro-expression in real time as it happens. Keep in mind the clues that have just been given as to what to look for and you should have success in reading what's happening beneath the expression on public display.

You would have to be consciously looking for a micro-expression in most cases to spot it. When doing so you will have to relinquish full attention upon what the person may be saying. To "catch" the nanosecond micro-expression you must be alert for it and it alone. But once you see it you will be rewarded with a truer knowledge of what the other person is communicating. Much more than mere words can offer. When you capture your first micro-expression you may be shocked by what you see because its content will most likely be completely unexpected. But by practicing this technique of micro-expression reading you will have found a way to decipher what a person is really feeling no matter what they may be saying.

If you can master this – and you should be able to – you will almost be able to read a person's subconscious and know how she TRULY feels. Once again, the secret is maintaining total vigilance on the face for that quick flash of expression that breaks in on the basic expression. It actually can be fun looking for a micro-expression because when you spot one it is so rewarding and revealing. But you must be single mindedly looking for it.

Micro-expressions are dealt with in detail in my book: "Micro-expressions: Reading Anyone's Hidden Thoughts."

Signs of Flirting

Flirting can be described as one person's attempt to attract the attention of another person for the purpose of potentially beginning a relationship based on more than friendship. In general men are constantly sending out signals toward any women of interest who will respond rather than the man focusing on one person in particular. Women, of course, are also proficient at flirting but usually more specifically directed.

Homosexual individuals as well as transgendered people have different forms of flirting which will be covered in another book.

Men make themselves available to any willing woman in various general ways. They make themselves obvious, if not conspicuous. This is done by assuming a posture that gives the appearance of enlarging the physical presence and by portraying a sense of masculinity. The series of photos below is a visual example of a man's flirting techniques.

Note above how the hands bracket the genital area and the feet are in a "waiting" posture and are completely different from a woman's "stay away" foot posture.

This is very similar but even more attracting. The hand behind the head (face not included by request) is a clear signal for attention like the **thumb outside the pocket**. The feet are spread in such a way as to welcome romantic contact.

The posture below is a clear call for action made by a supremely confident male.

The arsenal for men is pretty consistent relying on the bigger-than-life posture. And, of course, the inviting smile.

Women's flirting tactics are quite different and frequently unrecognized by the male because they are sometimes too subtle. Thus, those of you who are in search of a relationship with a female take close notice of the common flirting signals that may be sent your way.

Flirting almost always begins with the initial eye contact, which will be long enough for the recipient to know that it wasn't a mistake.

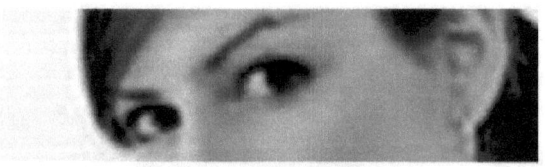

At this point, the sender of the signal will look quickly away. And this is where most of the opportunities are lost. The intended recipient loses further eye contact and misses the return gaze made by the female which is meant to let him know she really is interested. It's usually an over the shoulder type of gaze but it can also be an upward looking one. Both are powerful.

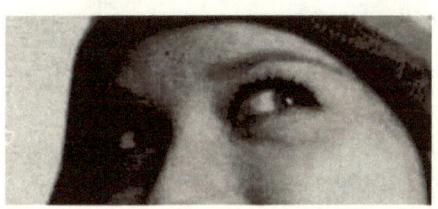

As mentioned earlier in this book, the head tilt offered by the female is very important. It is doubly attracting when accompanied by any type of hair stroking, but not scratching.

The next positioning is very important because it shows the fleshy under part of the arm which is known to be alluring. And hair stroking, too!

Additional calls for observation are the well placed hands near the thighs (below).

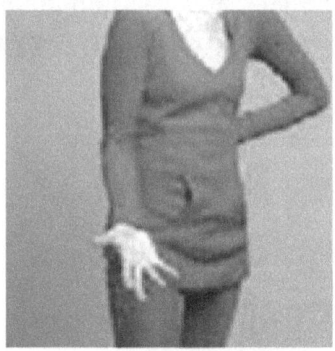

Once all of these various measures have been taken, a very obvious summons with a pucker and over the shoulder glance shouldn't leave anyone wondering.

(from an ad)

In reality, many men are so unattuned to the less blatant of signals, a woman may actually have to resort to so obvious a technique as that pictured above.

When the eye contact or other signals have been successful the space barrier between the two people involved will be lessened.

At this point, the female may begin performing what is meant to seem as clothing readjustments or the removal of foreign objects from her target's clothing. This **is** what it seems: she **is** initiating closer physical contact.

Other important signals to be aware of are lip moistening and /or parting which represents certain female erogenous zones. Another very important sign is when a woman dangles her foot outside of her shoe. None of these are accidental activities. They are all signals.

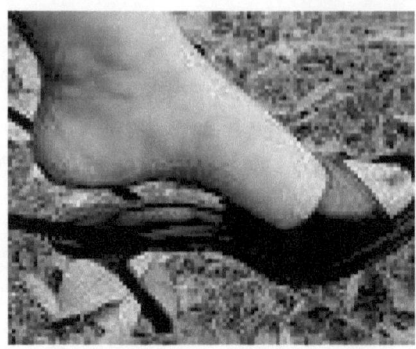

And, finally, one of the most suggestive and alluring of flirtatious behaviors is the female leg twine.

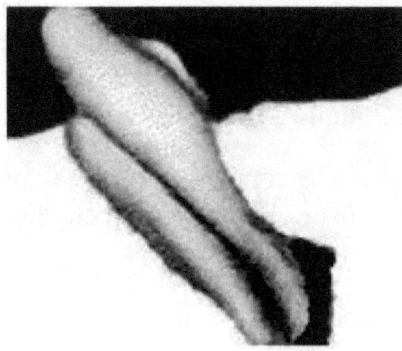

These are the basic signs of flirtation to be aware of that are used by females to attract a partner. The male basically uses larger-than-life methods to make himself more physically visible.

People to Avoid

People who are anti-social and who have psychopathic tendencies can be identified by their facial expressions, or lack thereof. These are the types who have no conscience and who show no remorse over causing harm. They are almost always identified by their blank, bland, emotion-free facial language. An enraged or incensed expression reveals emotion, feeling. But psychopaths lack genuine emotion which is why expressions of rage and anger are not common to them.

Psychopaths are not to be confused with a common type of bad tempered, angry or even hateful person. Psychopaths have no ability to feel these things and thus do not express them. Just cold detachment. To them, certain people are nothing more than obstacles to be overcome.

Below is the face of a psychopath.

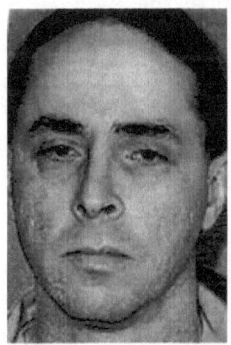

This is not an ordinary face. The qualities that make it different from an "average" angry type person are clear – lack of any feeling. Most psychopaths share these features.

Note the eyes very closely. What is missing?

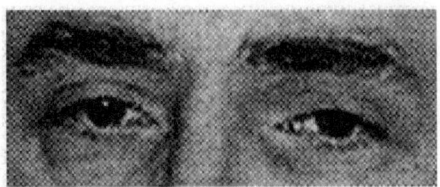

These eyes do not show rage. They don't show hatred. They have absolutely no emotion connected to them at all. They belong to a person who is devoid of human feeling and who lacks a sense of conscience.

This is not simply the face of an emotionless person. There are many people who have what are called deadpan faces and simply do not show a great deal of feeling. The face of this convicted cold-blooded murderer goes far beyond that.

Look not only at the eyes of a psychopath but also at the lower third of the face from the bottom of the nose to the end of the chin.

There is a complete lack of animation. The word soulless comes to mind. It could belong to a storefront dummy.

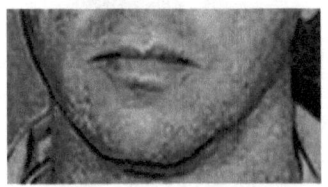

Below are the eyes of another bona-fide psychopath who committed a brutal murder.

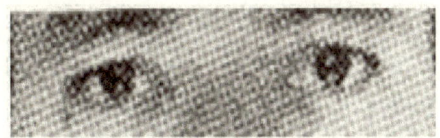

Next is the lower portion of the face.

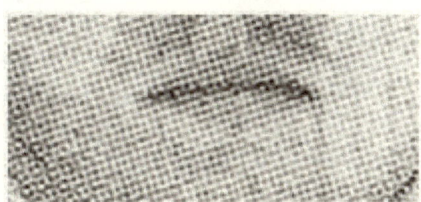

No lines, just a blank face. A face without animation. Just coincidence? Compare the first two psychopath's lower faces. See a similarity?

The eyes of a psychopathic woman show the same lack of feeling.

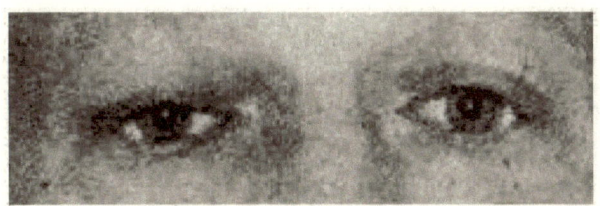

The features that are being singled out are the LACK OF emotion. Have you ever felt as if someone was "looking through you?" That should be an immediate warning. It's the opposite feeling of that had when a person is stabbing you with his eyes. The person who stabs with the eyes is also a person to be feared, but he is more obvious and not necessarily psychopathic.

There are two other major types of psychopathic facial features of which you should be aware. One of these is the quizzical gaze. It's as if the person looking at you isn't sure if you are confronting him by just being present.

There is this third type of psychotic face for which one has to be especially alert. It is the one of captivating, disarming charm.

Just be warned, psychotic faces are many and usually clearly show a mindless detachment from reality. The "charmers" are so adept at fooling others into believing that they are trustworthy that they believe it themselves and can transfer this belief to their own expressions. Thus, they seem charmingly innocent. Be warned.

Hopefully, this section has been helpful in giving a warning about the types of faces that are common to psychotics. The similarities are not coincidences, but they are as yet not fully understood.

Real Time Analysis

The purpose of this section is for you to practice evaluating body and facial language in real time – as you are approaching your target person – and determine his or her degree of openness to communication at this time. A series of photos will be shown and you will use these to rate the person in question. Is this person favorable or not favorable for communicating with at this time?

EXAMPLE:

If the person you are about to meet is in a stance similar to the one above he is most likely to be in an approachable mood. But, if the person looks like the one in the photo below, there might be a better time to speak to this person.

This does not mean that you should not contact the person it simply means that you should do so expecting the person to be in the mood he is displaying.

The purpose is to practice making your judgment quickly because in real time you will not have long to decide. Remember, because a person may not be in a favorable mood for communicating with at the moment this does not mean that his mood cannot change. And you may be instrumental in changing that mood through your own body and facial language.

Good Luck. The correct answers will follow immediately after the test.

BEGIN

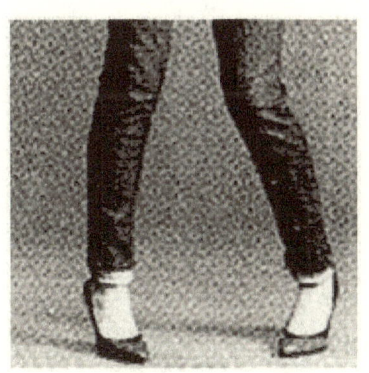

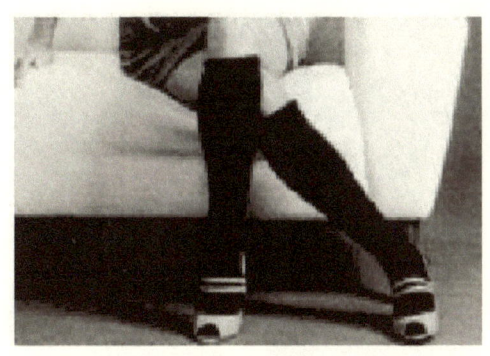

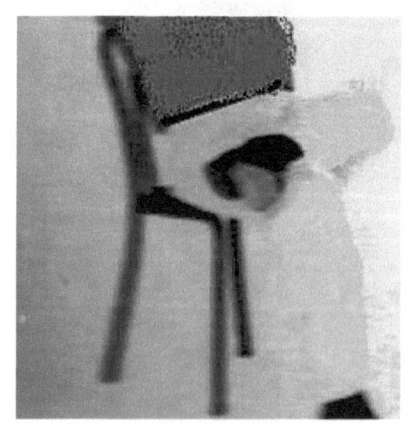

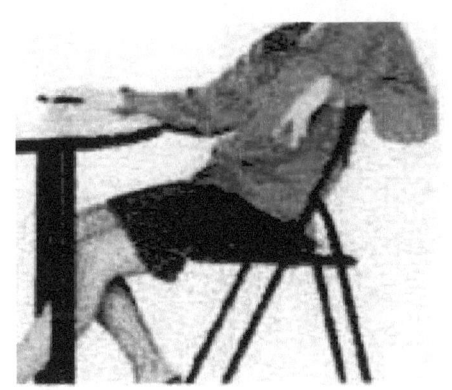

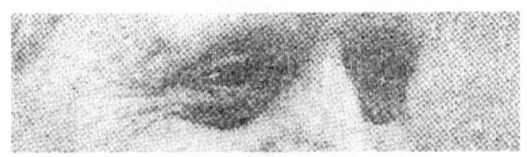

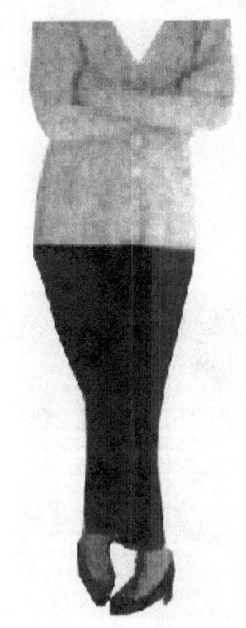

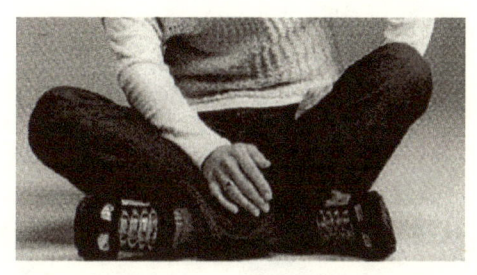

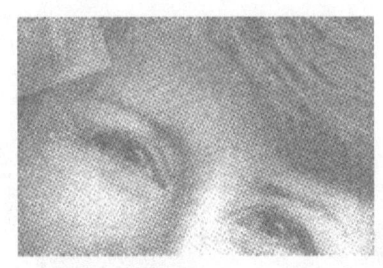

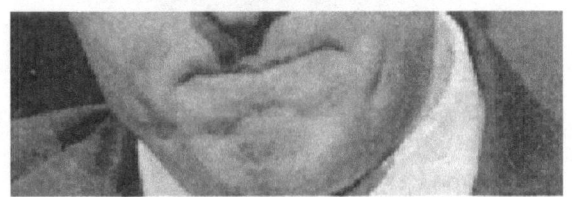

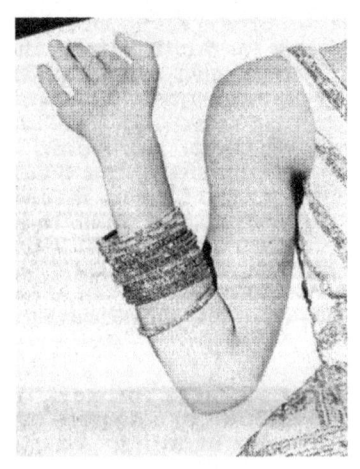

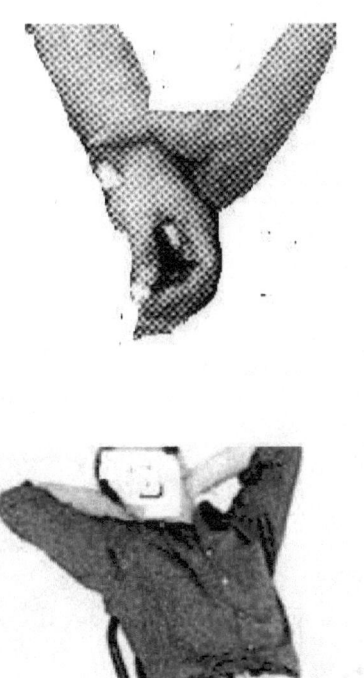

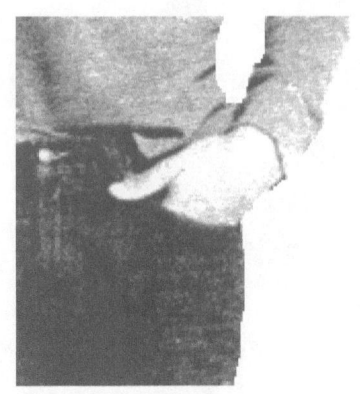

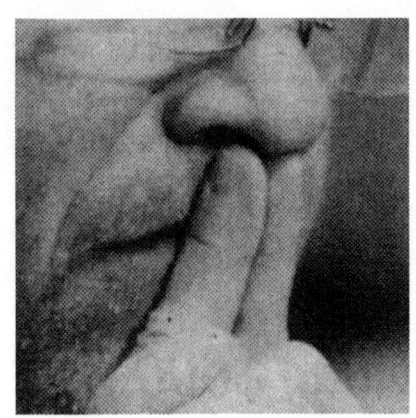

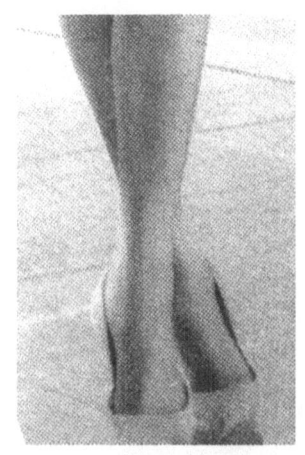

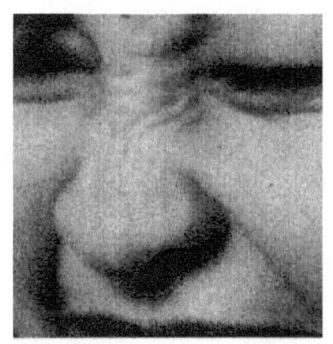

ANSWERS:

Approachable – palms openly raised, inviting.

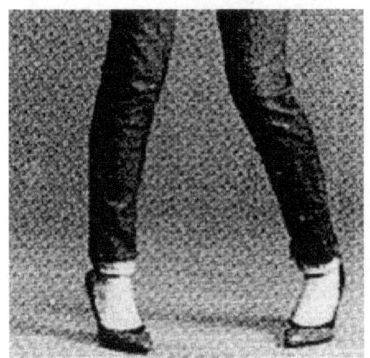

Confused, bordering on panic.

Highly self-assured. Approachable, but self-centered.

Undecided, hand welcoming but back leg withdrawn. Need more information (facial language).

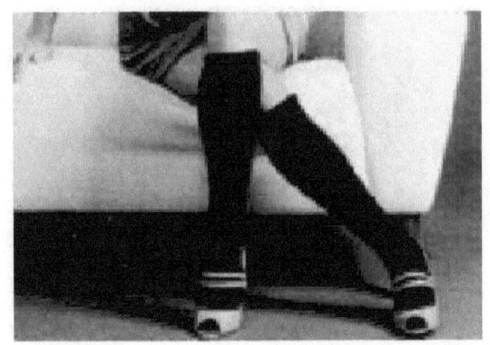

Under great stress, wishes to flee.

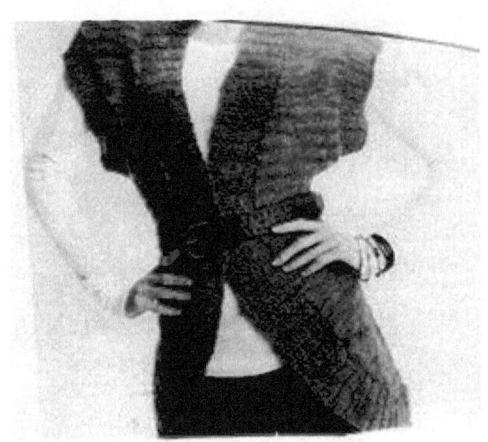

Stay away from me.

Stay away from me, too.

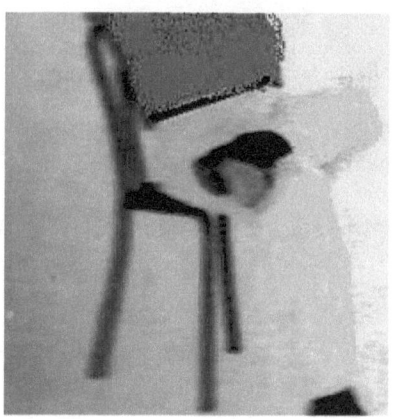

Not too open, blocking with foot, but potential friend.

Open to contact, with thumb exposed. Self assured.

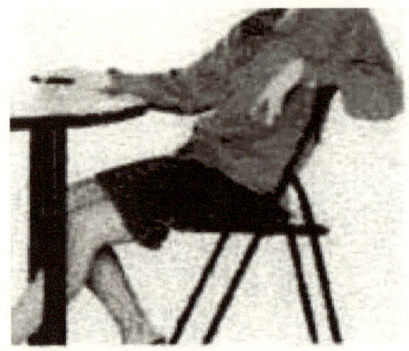

Very relaxed with self, comfortable body, potential friend.

Not too approachable – stiffly raised palms (even though upturned) and hooked fingers. Offset by clear distress in lower face.

Highly approachable. Flirtatious, dipped head, flashy forearms.

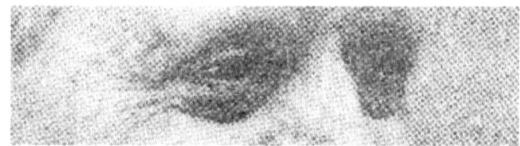

Friendly, if hard to see, smile around eyes.

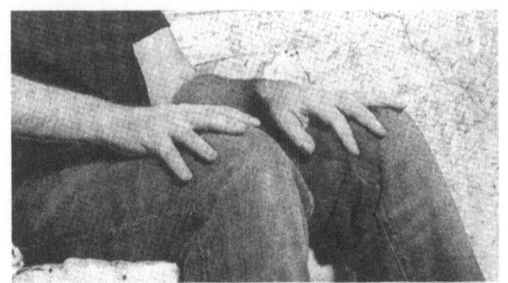

Tense, palms pressed onto knees.

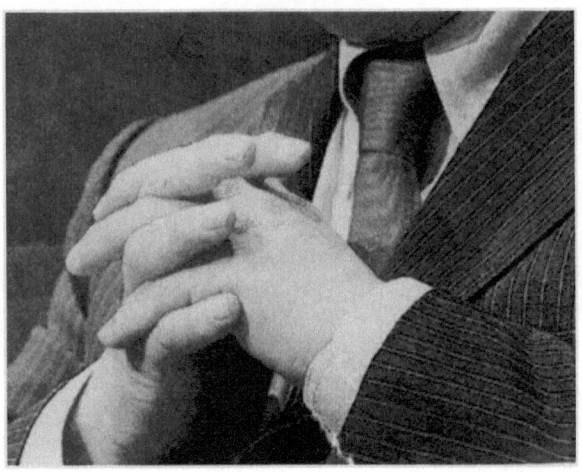

Very tense, hands twined in knotting.

Cautiously friendly, hands dangle in front.   Unsure.

Stay back!   Arms tightly crossed.   Feet and legs crossed.

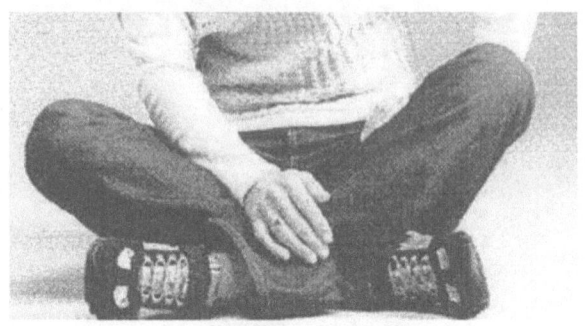

Seductive with hand placement, friendly.

Very friendly, hand behind head, open thumb from pocket.

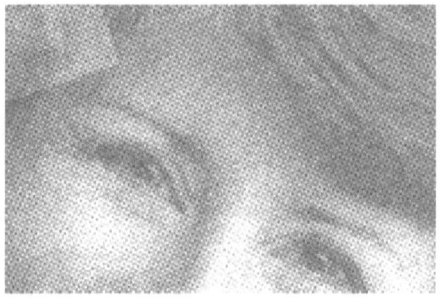

Welcoming with a true smile of the eyes in tilted head.

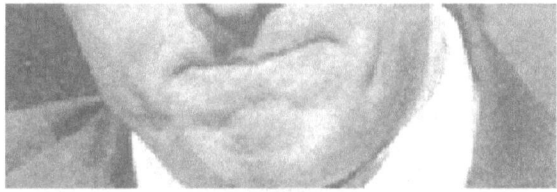

Would like to say more, but very, very tensely holding it in.

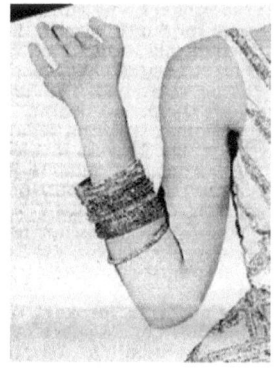

Very open, showing full forearm and palm splayed back.

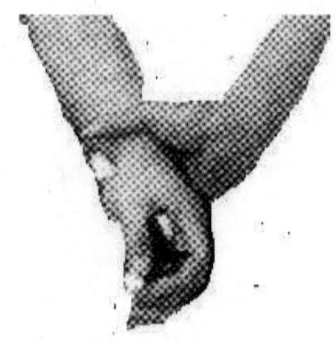

Hands tied behind back, not wanting contact.

Very open to contact with hands both behind head and sitting back.

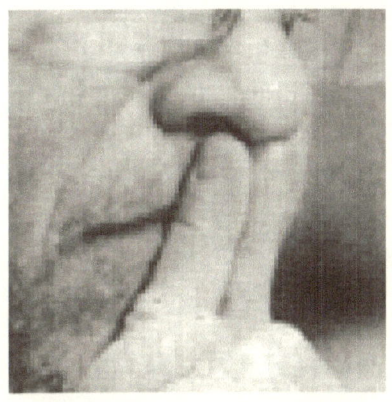

Tensely hiding information.

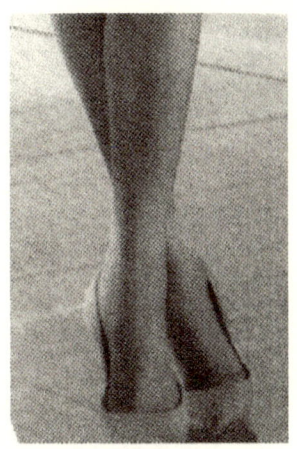

Very nervous, showing crossed ankles. Stay away!

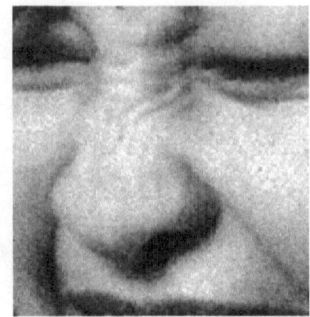

Disgust. Crinkled nose.

Applying it all

Applying it all means what it implies. This is the chapter devoted to putting to use what was covered in the earlier chapters, including staying away from dogs that appear in the distance to be friendly but really aren't.

One intention of this book was to introduce you to various types of non-verbal language commonly used by social aggressors and other difficult people and how to disarm them with body language of one form or another.

Non-verbal language is like spoken language in almost all ways. They both have rules that are consistent and don't change very much and are learned at an early age and remain in effect throughout life. Both types of languages can be learned as well as how to interpret and tailor one's own messages for one's own purposes. Always keep in mind that most body language is instinctively interpreted by the observer so – though she does not know exactly why – she responds a certain way to something you did.

In this upcoming segment, various body and facial language movements are shown and interpreted. What signals are these people below giving and how would you or how would you not incorporate them in the future? Assume that these people have just been asked what could possibly be an incriminating question.

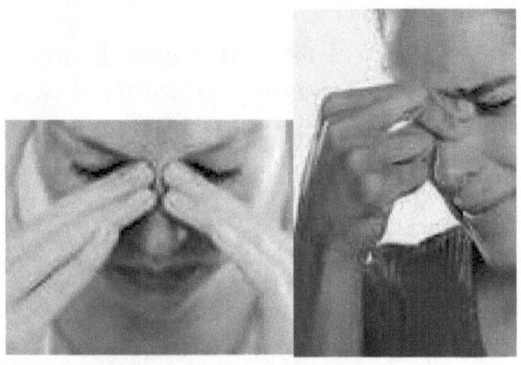

Did the dog scratching the back of his neck give it away? If you don't know what the meaning behind these peoples' non-verbal language is, here's one more clue.

Remember, the commonly held belief is that a person can decipher the truth or fiction of another's statements based on the direction his eyes are moving when replying. I don't believe it is viable because it is based on the left brain/right brain principle and which side controls the person being questioned. How can anyone possibly know with certainty which side of the brain is dominant with any particular stranger without first subjecting her to an MRI or something equivalent? And even with that knowledge, the basic theory is flawed with far too many variables.

So, the women in the photos above were attempting to not answer a particular question that was put to them and in the process they were disclosing untruthful behavior. By the way, men make the same physical responses.

When being interviewed for any reason, would the best advice be: to sit bolt upright and stare ahead like a mannequin?

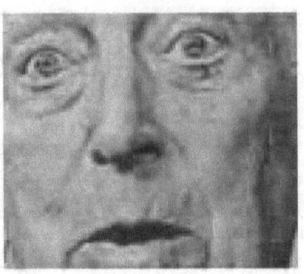

Or to just let your eyes fall where they may?

The correct answer is to just let your eyes fall where they may (within reason).

Return to the earlier photos of the women who were fiddling with noses and ears. This is something a person wants to avoid doing but if you find yourself unconsciously performing these motions take note of it. They are non-verbal signs of deception or attempted deception which it might be better for you to acknowledge to yourself. After all, we are all human. Do you recall the physiological reason why a person fiddles with the areas of the body just noted?

It is because these parts of the body tend to redden or change color when someone is in the process of telling an untruth and the person in question is unknowingly trying to hide this shade change. This applies to the back of the neck as well as to the nose.

There are other signals as well. For example, beware of the person who grabs hold of the arms of his chair and sits as far back from you as possible. It's a form of trying to escape the questioning. If the chair has wheels, he may even try to roll away.

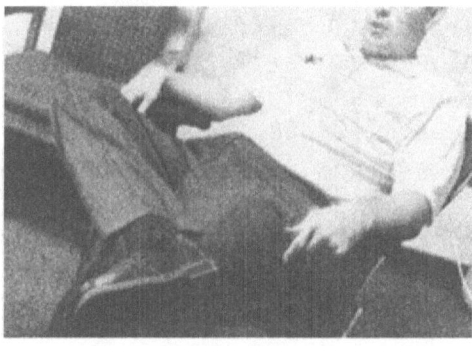

The leg crossed in the above manner is also a barrier put up against questioners. While this person may seem at ease and comfortable, that isn't what the cues are telling us. So, beware when you see it. And beware if you do it unless you're just being comfortable in that position. Always check all of the variables.

Is there a question or two that makes you uncomfortable? This is a good way to judge your own reactions to a situation. What is it about the conversation that might be upsetting you? This isn't to imply dishonesty, just uneasiness. But remember, a person can change his posture and give different non-verbal messages at any time.

Now that we've determined some of the primary cues that reveal potential deceit, what clues might imply that someone is truly thinking something over and not trying to avoid the matter?

Let's try a couple of examples.

Hmmm, thinking (both above and below)

Yes, these types of poses belong to people who are seriously considering something that had been proposed to him. Touching of the lips and chin in this manner tells us that.

It's just a natural thing for a person to rub the chin, side of the face or bottom of the lips when honestly considering something as is the individual below.

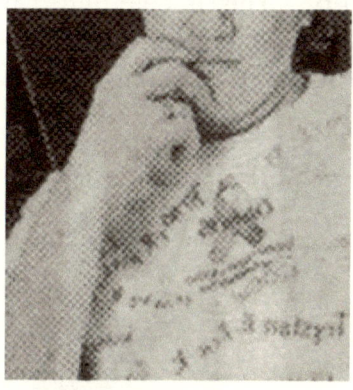

This thinker has pretty much covered the entire area. Side of face, lips and chin.

Let's turn to another facet of body language. Do

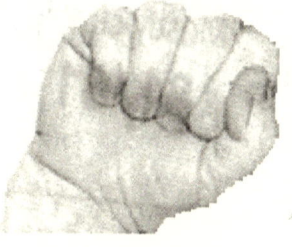

you remember the primary purpose of fists?

Knocking on doors? Yes, in a sense. What the fist does is to attract attention. It can be by knocking on doors or by being such an outstanding non-verbal cue as to demand that attention be given.

But just as there are many kinds of doors and ways to knock on them there are many types of fists. There are fists like the one above whose purpose is to proclaim some form of victory. This is determined by the way that the thumb is drawn into the side of the finger beside it and not drawn across it like in the picture below.

See the difference. This is a hard fist with the thumb crossing the two closest fingers. This is a fist of power. One that says, "I will beat you down."

And then there are the jubilant fists thrust skyward with joy.

The fist on the right appears to be one that implies anger, though, doesn't it? Almost. Why almost? Because it isn't drawn tightly down against the other fingers but it is lightly hovering over them. It more likely denotes uncertainty.

It is hoped that your fists be those of joy, even if subdued, like below.

But try not to become so happy with yourself that you tear a muscle by patting yourself on the back.

And never attempt this following maneuver unless quadruple jointed. Note the positioning of the hands closely. How did she possibly accomplish this?

Forearms also play a role in body language but are seldom mentioned. They are often used in conjunction with another person for the purpose of sharing joy over a project well done. Note below:

The woman's arm is raised in mild jubilation (the background of this picture is known to the author which is how it is known to be a double victory for these two). And also:

The same situation here. The raised forearm is a sign of a shared job well done by these two.

Do you recall ever sharing a victory with a partner like this? If you should be across the room observing this type of pose you may now have a better understanding of its meaning. It should be pointed out, however, that it is primarily a female trait.

The forearms are also used as one of the most formidable of body language devices for intimidation by bullies. It is the crossed arms at chest level.

The ways to disarm this stance are: move to the side of this person and keep moving while his arms loosen, or step up to a higher level using a stool, stair, or other object. His arms will drop looser when he has to peer upward. Do whichever makes logical sense.

The hands of course play one of the most important parts in the transmission of body language. One of the most significant is in the matter of handshakes. Have you ever thought of how you shake hands and why?

There are many types of handshakes and, as noted, they are more of a competitive device than a simple social gesture. Many people use the handshake to take charge of the conversation and ensuing relationship. It usually starts with the handshake.

Just keep in mind the basic point of the handshake. Only you can decide how you want to relate to the other person.

When considering body language the term lip reading takes on a different meaning from its normal usage.

What you are really doing is deciphering what the other person IS NOT saying. This is particularly prominent in politics. For example, when you see a pair of lips pressed together like this:

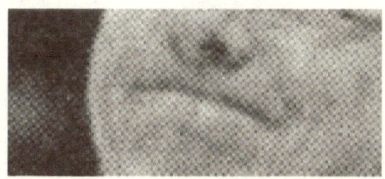

you are being silently told that the speaker would like to say a lot of things to you but that he won't. It is a way of saying that he will speak only of nonimportant items. If you ask anything that might reveal some crucial information it will be evaded.

Basically, these types of compressed lips all have the same concept in common: withholding information and not necessarily in a negative way. When reading them in micro-expression form these types of lips are in effect suppressing a shout. The speaker is either so angry or hurt by something that he holds his lips tightly together as if to keep from yelling.

Reading a person's hand gestures is somewhat similar. The basic idea is that when the palms are upturned this means that the person is open to discussion and finding compromise. But note the fingers. If they are hooked, compromise may not be under consideration.

Take that same palm pointing upward and flip it over into the claw position, this would show a decidely non-compromising gesture:

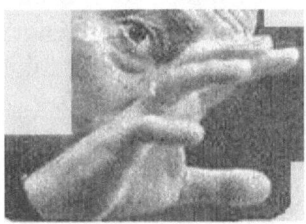

And some people use the double claw attack:

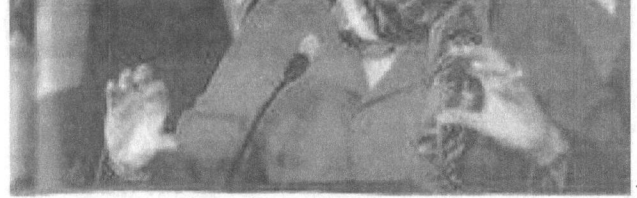 to stress their point.

There isn't any right or wrong. The important point is to get your true signal read.

Note the following images and the messages that accompany the body language.

Is the following what you would mean to say :

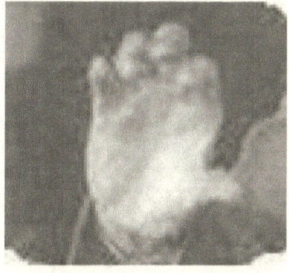

"No more discussion!" (claw)

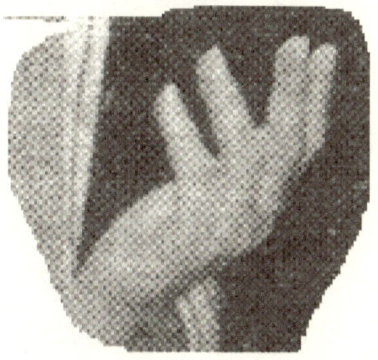

Let's talk. (fingers splayed not hooked)

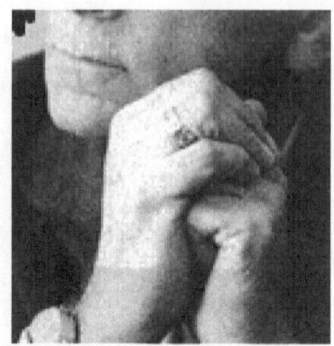

I'm really tense right now.

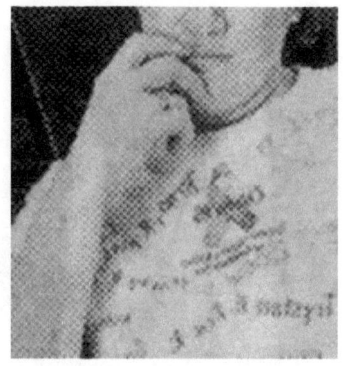

Yes, I will consider your idea.

Ow!

Looking for my quarter.

All right, I'll give you a chance to talk. (arms folded at waist height, not chest level)

Here I am and I'm staying awhile.

I'm not sure how I feel about this. (one hand in pocket, one hand out dangling free). But I am self-assured about myself.

This is grass.

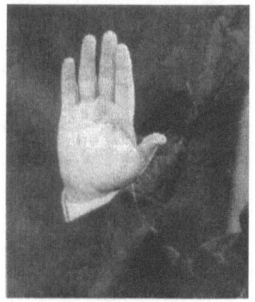

I seem to have enough testosterone (length of ring finger).

I'm not telling you anything else. (pen in hand as barrier in addition to crossed fingers)

I'm superior to you and am keeping my secrets to myself. Though I am tense.

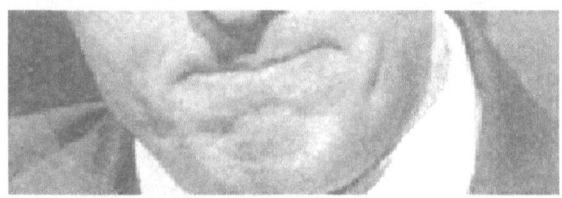

Oh, what I'd like to say (suppressed shout).

How do you ride this thing?

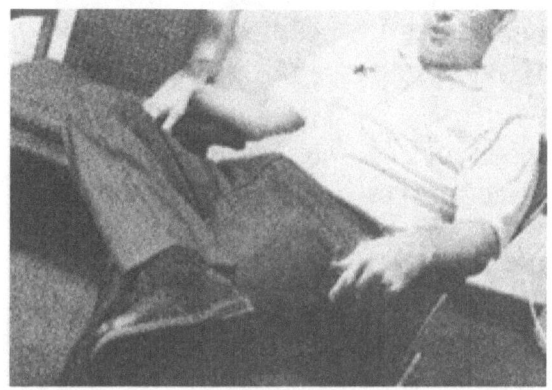

I'm planted here and ain't telling you anything.

I'm listening but I am getting a little bored (chin resting in palm).

Yes! We succeeded. (arm across chest and fist made). But, don't want to talk right now (glass-in-hand barrier).

Don't just sit there like a statue.

I will pound you!

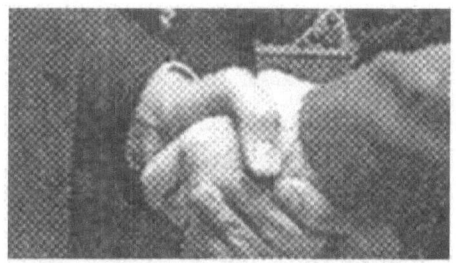

I will control you!

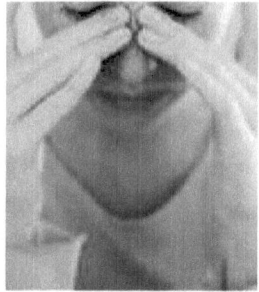

I didn't eat your chocolate ice cream.

You can use your own body language to control situations, especially those involving intimidators and bothersome people. You truly can change opinions and viewpoints with your own body language. Try the simple smile test. See how many people favorably respond. Try a different type of handshake and see how the other person reacts. If you give the correct non-verbal cue for what you intend to "say" the chances are highly in your favor that it will be correctly read.

Finally

You may have noticed that much of reading body and facial language is common sense. Intuition is involved, too, since most people can sense deceit when confronted with it.

An important thing to remember is that a person's mood is subject to change. A person whose body language may be hostile one day may be the opposite the next due to changes that have occurred to him over the past twenty four hours.

Also important to remember is that there are many signals being displayed indicating a person's state of mind and as many signs as possible have to be taken into account to perform an accurate reading.

You might want to be aware that you too are giving off signals with your body and facial language and the other person can be reacting to them. In fact, you can use your knowledge of these signs to create the environment you want. If you want to charm a person a genuine smile is the way to do it. If you want to maintain distance, close yourself off with folded arms and legs crossed pointing away from the other person. If you want to remain neutral dangle your arms at your sides and keep feet parallel but closely so.

If you really want to impress someone and attract him to you - give a visible eyebrow flash. (Remember the genuine one is a micro-expression). But it must be performed so quickly that he doesn't consciously notice it. See what happens.

Please take very seriously the section about the psychopathic indicators. These are people to avoid at all costs.

Try to develop the ability to read micro-expressions. This is the truest and shortest way into a person's subconscious.

You have the basic tools now at your disposal. This means that you can start reading people like a book. Start with the cover.

One More Thing

In early 2010 a picture of a composite figure was released which was supposed to represent the perfect representative face for humanity.

The same thing had been done in the late 19th century. Below is the picture of what is supposed to represent the perfect representative face of humanity (only male, of course) in the 1890's.

WHO WOULD FIT THIS FRAME TODAY (male AND female)?

Thanks for reading.

THE END

www.ingramcontent.com/pod-product-compliance
Lightning Source LLC
Chambersburg PA
CBHW030442300426
44112CB00009B/1120